David Parsons

T0311270

DEMYSTIFYING EVALUATION

Practical approaches for researchers and users

POLICY PRESS SHORTS POLICY & PRACTICE

First published in Great Britain in 2017 by

Policy Press
University of Bristol
1-9 Old Park Hill
Bristol
BS2 8BB
UK
t: +44 (0)117 954 5940
pp-info@bristol.ac.uk
www.policypress.co.uk

North America office:
Policy Press
c/o The University of Chicago Press
1427 East 60th Street
Chicago, IL 60637, USA
t: +1 773 702 7700
f: +1 773 702 9756
sales@press.uchicago.edu
www.press.uchicago.edu

British Library Cataloguing in Publication Data
A catalogue record for this book is available from the British Library.

Library of Congress Cataloging-in-Publication Data
A catalog record for this book has been requested.

ISBN 978-1-4473-3390-6 (paperback)
ISBN 978-1-4473-3392-0 (ePub)
ISBN 978-1-4473-3393-7 (Mobi)
ISBN 978-1-4473-3391-3 (ePDF)

Cover design by Policy Press
Image: iStock

Printed and bound by CPI Group (UK) Ltd, Croydon, CR0 4YY

Contents

List of figures

List of examples

Acknowledgements

This book is long overdue; 30 years of my practice in programme and impact evaluation has yielded numerous client reports but not a single written reflection on methodologies. It took a consultation among members or the UK's Social Research Association (SRA) to identify the need for a book to demystify evaluation and the suggestion from Graham Farrant to Policy Press that I should write it. My thanks also go to the many participants of evaluation courses I have run for SRA and many others on their experiences of where they felt challenged in moving from current literature, and theory, into practice. Their shared insights have contributed much to the decisions on what to focus on in the book, and what to leave for others.

Many colleagues, too many to name individually, as well as clients, have been encouraging and at times patient, but I would like to draw attention to David Devins, Rhodri Thomas and Kenneth Walsh, especially for their consistently helpful and constructive comments. My editor at Policy Press, Rebecca Tomlinson, has been patient and always encouraging as the book has been dragged across four different countries while it progressed from concept to drafting.

I save my final acknowledgement for Dorothy Smith, my wife and partner in practice. She has laboured long, hard and with infinite patience as principal (and unpaid) copy editor to ensure my narrative enthusiasms have remained on the straight and narrow. Over several months she has provided constant encouragement, especially through the dark days of ensuring that a book aimed at a 'Shorts Series' did not become the contradiction in terms that it once seemed it might.

Preface

Evaluation methods and the plethora of theories surrounding them can be mystifying for the uninitiated. It does not have to be that way.

This book aims to help students, researchers, professionals, practitioners and anyone else coming new or inexperienced to evaluation, as specifiers, designers or users, to cut through the jargon. Its approach is practical, not theoretical, and its starting point is the dilemma set out a quarter of a century ago by Michael Scriven, the British-born, Australian polymath and philosopher, who said:

> Practical life cannot proceed without evaluation, nor can intellectual life, nor can moral life, and they are not built on sand. The real question is how to do evaluation well, not to avoid it. (Scriven, 1991, p 8)

A past president of the American Evaluation Association, Scriven's *how* vs *if* challenge drew on four decades of practical experience and an already deep legacy of evaluation developments in health, life and physical sciences. Social science has come relatively late to this challenge, and has been slow to resolve its discomfort with how well the evaluation legacy from other disciplines fits the social world. Much of the methodological confusion, and many of what at first may seem contradictory theories facing new evaluators today, stem from this.

This is not to say that the evaluation toolbox remains empty; many social scientists facing their first cautious steps into design, delivery or use of evaluation might think it is overfull. What is needed is not a more compact toolbox but a practical and joined-up way of thinking about how the tools available best fit different needs and circumstances. For perhaps two decades or more, social scientists in North America and Northern Europe in particular have been struggling with trying to define this, often from the standpoint of their own disciplines. The extensive literature that has resulted has been scholarly, often thought-provoking and sometimes influential, but outside the sphere of experienced evaluators and academics this has too often added to confusion, not diminished it.

If confusion was not enough, the demands today on evaluators have accelerated exponentially. Social scientists working in policy and practice find that 'doing evaluation well' brings challenges that could not have been anticipated 25 years ago. Decision makers' timeframes for evidence collection and analysis shrink; budgets diminish; more and more is expected for less, and in less time. It is not going too far to say that evaluators today face making design choices in a 'perfect storm' of rising expectations and diminishing resources.

This book does not propose some new paradigm of evaluation in social science as a readymade answer to these and other challenges. Its starting point is that these challenges can be faced, and addressed, but only if we are not wedded to particular theoretical approaches and are prepared to think outside (and across) narrow disciplinary perspectives. Past cross-disciplinary practice is our instructor in this guide; viable tools and techniques abound and their different strengths and weaknesses can be readily mapped and (often) easily grasped. All this can be harnessed by those with some social research understanding to demystify evaluation. From that standpoint, they will be well placed to start to make confident and appropriate evaluation choices, rising to Scriven's challenge by answering a similar one set out by Ovretveit:

> The question is no longer whether we use or make an evaluation; but how well we use or carry one out. (Ovretveit, 1997, p 1)

Glossary of selected evaluation terms

Additionality: The net measured or observed changes to outcomes or impacts from an intervention over and above what was expected.

Attribution: Analysis within impact evaluation which determines the extent to which the intervention being assessed was responsible for outcomes and impacts being measured.

Before and after analysis: A non-empirical method of measuring counterfactual evidence (see below), which quantitatively contrasts observed outcomes for selected impact indicators during or after an intervention, with directly parallel data on the same indicators before the intervention took place.

Blinded evaluation: A blind, or blinded, evaluation is characteristic of experimental approaches and typically randomised controlled trials (RCTs) where as a control measure to minimise bias, information about the test is masked from the participant until after the evaluation outcome is known.

Causal analysis: An analysis that isolates that part of an observed impact from an intervention that can be directly attributed to the implementation (set against other influences on change).

Comparative group (and analysis): A method of impact evaluation which assesses causality by contrasting observed outcomes or impacts in an intervention group with a closely matched comparison group such as a like-for-like geographical area, typically in a quasi-experimental evaluation.

Control group (and analysis): A method of impact evaluation which assesses causality of observed outcomes or impacts related to an intervention by establishing a systematic comparative analysis of change in a structured, matched, randomly selected non-intervention group, typically in an RCT.

Counterfactual analysis: An analysis within an evaluation design which identifies what would have occurred if an intervention or activity had not been implemented and compares this to the measured outcomes after the intervention. This alternate reality is called the 'counterfactual'.

Deadweight: An identified effect within an intervention which supports some of measured outcome or impact. This is an important feature for isolating 'net' from gross 'impacts' (see below).

Gross value/impact: An overall and non-attributed outcome or impact resulting from an (evaluated) intervention or activity (see impact below).

Hybrid evaluation: An evaluation methodology using a mixed mode approach and typically combining quantitative and qualitative methods to triangluate (see below) different evidence perspectives or sources.

Impact: An observed effect resulting from an (evaluated) intervention and as a consequence of delivering or achieving specific activities or 'outputs'. It is usually associated with measurement of intended medium- or longer-term consequential changes.

Knock-on impact: An unexpected, unintended or indirect consequential effect of an (evaluated) intervention (see impact above).

Leakage: Effects within measured outcomes or impacts which support others outside the targeted or expected intervention group.

Monetised: The process that results in an outcome or impact being converted or translated into a quantified cash or financial value.

Net value/impact: An outcome or impact attributed to a specific intervention or activity which discounts changes that would have otherwise occurred without the (evaluated) intervention or activity having taken place.

Neutral assessment: An approach to evaluation design and conduct which encourages robust separation of evaluators from the process of what is being evaluated and (pre-reporting) from users.

Opportunity cost: A benefit, profit or value of something that must be given up to acquire or achieve something else; the *next best alternative foregone.*

Outcomes: An early or short-term effect resulting from an (evaluated) intervention and usually resulting as a consequence of delivering or achieving specific activities or 'outputs' (see also impact above).

Participatory evaluation: An approach to evaluation conduct based on, but narrower than, participatory action research (PAR) principles, which provides opportunities for evaluators to put stakeholders, including beneficiaries, centre stage in evidence collection and review.

Primary evidence: Quantitative and/or qualitative evidence in an evaluation which is generated directly by the evaluator (or on their behalf) from additional information collection methods.

Proportionality: The principle of evaluation design which sets out that in addition to the need for reliable information, the choice and mixture of evidence gathering and analytical methods to be used should be 'proportionate' to the objectives, scale and nature of the programme being evaluated.

Secondary evidence: Quantitative and/or qualitative evidence in an evaluation which is collated from existing sources of evidence within or outside an intervention including from, for example, management or monitoring information and diverse documentary sources.

Sensitivity analysis: Analysis of the effects on an evaluation of different assumptions, including varying the projected values of important variables.

Small 'n' evaluation: A small scale evaluation where 'n' relates to the overall size and scope of participation in what is being evaluated, perhaps in a trial scheme, small-scale pilot, highly localised or single-site intervention, or one involving a narrow or specialised beneficiary group.

Social Return on Investment: SROI is a specialised method developed first in the area of social enterprise and building on cost-benefit analysis aimed at valuing social and environmental impacts from initiatives and actions, which may not be fully covered in more conventional approaches to economic evaluation.

Spill-over effects: Unplanned consequences arising from (evaluated) interventions and activities and which can be positive (adding to the quality and range of expected impacts) or negative (detracting from programme achievements and impacts).

Substitution: Measured outcomes or impacts (or aspects of them) on an intervention group which are realised at the expense of others outside the intervention group, often as unintended consequences of the intervention (see below).

Triangulated evidence: Triangulation is a commonly used approach in all forms of evaluation that provides for validation of both quantitative and qualitative evidence through cross-verification from two or more sources, typically derived from combination of several research methods in assessing the same phenomenon.

Unintended consequences: Unexpected impacts and effects of (evaluated) interventions and activities which need to be identified and taken into account in any assessment of net impacts (see also spill-over effects).

Valuation: Techniques for measuring or estimating the monetary and/or non-monetary value (see above) of observed outcomes and impacts, contributing to an assessment of added value or cost-effectiveness of the evaluated intervention.

Value for money: Value for money (VFM) measures the extent to which an intervention (or sets of activities) has provided the maximum benefit for funding bodies from the resourcing of activities, benefits secured and outcomes and impacts arising. VFM provides a quantitative measure, typically for specific goods or services, or combinations of these.

1

INTRODUCTION

- Why demystify evaluation; why should it be more accessible?
- Who can the book help; who is the book aimed at?
- What is evaluation, how it is different from research and where are its roots?
- Why evaluate? Generating evidence for accountability, development and knowledge
- When to evaluate? Using ex ante, ex post, formative and summative evaluations
- The three 'Cs' of evaluation and using them to get the most from the book

Why 'demystifying' evaluation?

Evaluation is not quite the exact 'science' that some may suggest. At its heart, an effective evaluation is about the quality of choices made in balancing realistic expectations and needs of it, with judgements about focus, scope and methods. These choices are not made any easier by an abundance of evaluation theories and methods, a surfeit of jargon, and practitioner guidance that too often seems aimed at the expert rather than the newcomer. All this can be mystifying for those new to the field, whether tasked with specifying an evaluation, designing and delivery it, interpreting the evidence or using the findings to guide decision makers.

Can we improve on this situation? My experience as both an evaluator and a user suggests that understanding evaluation, and making sound choices about methods and approach, is within the scope of any social scientist (social science being the main focus of this book) who has at least a grasp of systematic research methods. That understanding comes from:

- a practical appreciation of what the evidence to be generated is to be used for (and how);
- the different practical options that might fit the evaluation circumstances and are best suited to generate that evidence;
- the respective advantages and disadvantages of those options;
- the pitfalls to watch out for in choosing and applying methods and how to avoid them.

The starting point for developing this understanding is cutting through the theories and reducing what may seem to be conflicting, even contradictory, approaches to ideas, language and options that can be readily understood – demystifying evaluation.

Why is it important to ensure that many more people have a better understanding of evaluation? Perhaps it is enough that a small cadre of 'experts' in evaluation put the time and effort into building this understanding, and applying it to the benefit of others. I believe not, and working in activities funded by the public sector, or in public interest occupations, increasingly means working knowledgably with evaluation (or evaluators) in some way. Those asked to help with or even undertake an evaluation of a project, policy or initiative will consequently find themselves caught up in a plethora of design and delivery options, and few, if any, 'experts' to lean on. Some may be asked to help set out or specify an evaluation for others to undertake, to select or manage external evaluators, or to join a team to steer an evaluation to a successful result.

The circumstances and roles are different, but as they start to explore what might be involved, many first time evaluators may be asking themselves questions like:

- How is evaluation different from research?
- What quantitative methods are 'best'; is there a role for qualitative evidence?
- How can limited time or money square with users' expectations of evaluation?
- What can be sensibly measured for impact; are outputs different from outcomes?
- How can we make an evaluation independent; do we need external evaluators?
- When is the best time to do it?

Questions like these stem from the great diversity of evaluation choices, and an almost infinite range of possible methods with what may at first seem to be conflicting or competing merits. So for many, the theory underlying the practice of evaluation needs interpretation if they are to engage with it constructively and confidently.

This book aims to help with this, not by focusing on a particular evaluation theory or approach, but by cutting across the range on offer to unpick the terminology, and see what evaluation is (and is not) about. By going back to some of the basics, it aims to help readers better understand what is appropriate, practical and achievable in the different evaluation needs and circumstances they will be facing. It is not designed to 'instruct' the reader on what to do, but to rather help them understand the issues that must be taken into consideration when designing and delivering evaluations of different kinds. The focus is on helping applied researchers and practitioners in many areas understand the realities of evaluation practice, the constraints they have to work within and the compromises that often have to be made – particularly given limited time and resources.

Who is the book for?

The book aims to help four groups of likely readers:

- those new, or relatively new, to evaluation looking to build their understanding and confidence about choosing and using practical approaches to evaluation;
- final year and postgraduate students coming to grips with evaluation for the first time, perhaps in dissertations or theses, or possibly considering a career in social or policy research;
- practitioners already in the evaluation community who, like many, have learned their trade largely by 'doing' and who are now looking for a more comprehensive introduction across different evaluation approaches;
- commissioners of evaluation, and various users helping decision makers to use evaluation evidence.

I have identified the need for a book to help each of these groups based on the practical experiences of many hundreds of practitioners and managers, from very different backgrounds, who have been drawn to the evaluation courses I have the privilege to run for the UK's Social Research Association (SRA) and others. Their experiences show that for all these groups there is a mystique surrounding evaluation, which confuses not only 'new' evaluators but also many other stakeholders (Weiss, 1998a) drawn from procurement, project management, programme delivery, policy analysis and advice.

These courses have also shown how many have been left wanting from the available books and guides aimed at explaining evaluation. Some of these guides can assume theoretical knowledge that readers from different backgrounds don't have. Others may be preoccupied with making the case for a particular evaluation concept or approach at the expense of a wider perspective on options and choices. And some are focused on very specific and often narrow evaluation contexts which may not be relevant to the newcomer. While there is much of potential value in much of this literature, its focus on the initiated too often hinders rather than helps those starting out in evaluation.

The book is a 'starter guide' for all these groups; one that can provide a bridge into some of the more detailed literature. To do this, it:

- provides a short, practically focused guide, looking across the wider field of evaluation within social contexts;
- sets out a plural review across different theories and methods in the social field, not limiting itself to any one methodological perspective;
- takes a nonaligned view of different methods, and their advantages and disadvantages;
- uses a series of practical illustrations and examples to highlight what works;
- provides critical insights on the pitfalls that need to be avoided when applying these methods to policy, programme and similar evaluation contexts.

It is a deliberately 'short' book, and does not give detailed 'how to' guidance on very specific methods, but leaves this to the technical guidance and references signposted through the text, and where there are already a number of excellent sources about specific methods or applications.

So what is evaluation?

Evaluation is not so difficult to grasp as an idea. We probably all do it in some fashion every day, or certainly every week of our lives. Consciously and more often unconsciously, we make judgements about commonplace and also less everyday things: what has worked, what could work better, what has been of value.

It is less commonplace to be doing this systematically, being guided in those judgements not by sense or feeling, or the views of others, but by evidence, collected rigorously and closely fitted to specific information needs. There are many formal definitions of evaluation from well-placed academics – so many that nearly 20 years ago an attempt was made at a comparative analysis across these (Clarke, 1999). Not all are helpful to those new to the field, with academic definitions in particular becoming more, not less complex. Personally, I like two drawn from outside academia:

> Evaluation is an objective process of understanding how a policy or other intervention was implemented, what effects it had, for whom, how and why. (HM Treasury, 2011, p 11)

> Evaluation is the systematic assessment of the design, implementation or results of an initiative for the purposes of learning or decision-making. (Poth et al, 2012; Canadian Evaluation Society, 2015)

These come from two different perspectives: the first, from guidance in the UK to central government project managers, analysts and civil servants working in many different areas; the second, from the Canadian professional body, which is drawing on a long-established association with programme evaluation. Looking across these, and as with other useful approaches to definition, they share an actual or implicit focus on evaluation being:

- structured and planned – not an ad hoc activity;
- objective and goal-centred;
- focused on gathering systematic evidence – and analysing it – for making specific judgements and decision-making (or learning).

Implicit in this, as one of the architects of programme evaluation makes clear (Weiss, 1998a), is a focus on contributing evidence for improvement. Others have more recently emphasised that evaluation produces results that are intended to be used (Mertens and Wilson, 2012).

These definitions are a better starting point than evaluation theory, especially in and around the social and economic world. This is not to say that there have not been evaluation theorists trying to set out a comprehensive framework of knowledge that can predict, explain and allow us to better understand what evaluation is about per se. The problem is rather that for those coming to systematic evaluation for the first time, there may seem to be too many theorists, often looking at slightly different things, and with what may at first sight seem inconsistent explanations. They may even gain the impression of different theorists whose ideas seem at odds, even competitive. As it stands, a unifying theory of evaluation in the social world remains rather elusive.

To go a little deeper, it is helpful to start with looking at what is usually evaluated and how evaluation as an idea has evolved.

Intervention and what is evaluated

Evaluation gathers data and other information for the purpose of informing required (and usually planned) decision-making about specific things. Those 'things' are incredibly varied, but most commonly focus on some form of *intervention* – perhaps a new initiative, programme or a new or modified policy – and are usually set up to tackle a specific need or challenge. So, while different interventions will have widely different goals, they share expectations that they will make a difference (for example, in people's lives) in some specific way.

Of course, evaluation will not be the only contribution to decision-making for an intervention. It will (too) often not even be the weightiest influence, but it will probably be the only one based on hard evidence of the changes coming out of the intervention, how these come about and their value set against needs and expectations. Without an appropriate evaluation, decision-making will be dependent on almost wholly subjective assessment, opinion or stakeholder influencing – not always the most reliable basis for good judgements.

It is this association between an intervention and informing decision-making that sets evaluation – and evaluators – apart from applied research. Both may be systematic and evidence-based, and as we shall see, many of the processes and methods may be very similar, but the purposes to which they are put are quite different. Reduced to a rather simplified essence, research in all its guises centres on improving knowledge and understanding, although it may also be expected to produce information or explanation that is useful to decision-makers or practitioners (for example, policy-related research). In contrast, while evaluation may well be tasked in part with understanding how things work (more) effectively, its end purpose is to provide evidence about a specific intervention to inform judgements or decision-making. Keeping this sense of focus and decision-making purpose is at the heart of planning, designing, managing and delivering an effective evaluation.

Evaluation origins and evolution

Reliable evaluation has come to have currency internationally, in and around all levels of government, regulatory and funding bodies. It has some early origins going back to Europe from the mid-seventeenth century, through Jefferson and others in North America, with the so called second phase of the scientific revolution giving impetus to new philosophical and political thought in the Age of Reason. These developments, philosophical and scientific, made the case for separation of exploration of evidence and establishment of facts from making moral or values-based judgements about meaning. Although distant, even obscure, foundations, they remain the roots for all of the theories and approaches now underpinning systematic evaluation.

In more modern times, different disciplines have tended to pursue rather different pathways towards evaluation. Some can trace ideas-building or key developments back to the earlier years of the twentieth century; others see developments coming a lot later. Few, however, would argue that modern evaluation grew from scientific and rational roots, even if some of these early foundations were not always explicit. As early as 1601, it was Sir James Lancaster, the English mariner, who performed, probably inadvertently, the first quasi-experimental evaluation (see Chapter 6) providing *empirical* evidence to support citrus as an active prevention for scurvy on long sea trips. Others followed (rather later) with experimental evaluation coming to the forefront in the medical and health disciplines, now institutionalised in drug and therapeutic trials.

While much of the now wider demand for evaluation, and especially impact evaluation, comes directly or indirectly from the public sector or from publicly financed initiatives, government was generally late in coming to systematic evaluation. For a long time, evidence-informed decision-making seems to have appealed more to those generating evidence than to government users. Even Sir James's scurvy 'evaluation' results took nearly another 200 years to have a direct effect on government (naval) policy after he first drew them to the attention of the British Admiralty.

Outside the early modern use of evaluation for drug and clinical regulation and health policy, governments have lagged behind wider business practice in using systematic evaluation. From the 1930s, evaluation methods in, for example, performance assessment and management were widely harnessed by the corporate sector in North America, and later in Western and Northern Europe. Yet it was only from the mid-1960s, and especially in North America as evaluation started to feature in MBA programmes, that this started to become a feature for assessing the results of publicly funded programmes, gaining greater currency from the 1970s.

Yet although late to embrace the role of evaluation in evidence-informed policy making, it was growing government demand for evaluation which led to the dramatic expansion in academic interests in methods, options and theorising for evaluation in the last part of the twentieth century, on which this books draws. Impact evaluation came particularly late to the government policy process but was given a substantial boost on both sides of the Atlantic in the 1990s by legislative reforms such as through the UKs *Modernising Government* White Paper (HMSO, 1999), moving governments away from looking at outputs of the programmes it funded to understanding their effects and effectiveness.

Despite coming late to the party, national governments, international bodies and others have now embraced systematic evaluation enthusiastically and widely. It is now commonly a central commitment of different political administrations, particularly in assessing the added value and effects of public investments and new regulation.

Why evaluate?

For some readers the question may seem irrelevant. When asking at the beginning of courses why people are conducting evaluations I have been known to hear: "Because we have to." For many experienced evaluators this 'must do' rationale was their first serious engagement with the field, often stemming from external finance for a project where evaluation was a condition of the funding. Elsewhere, it may also be a contractual obligation built into, for example, partnership activity.

However, the 'must do' rationale is only a part of the picture. Getting under the skin of why an evaluation needs to be conducted is the first in a series of questions that those charged with kick-starting it must get to grips with. One explanation of 'why evaluate' (Chelimsky and Shadish, 1997) has synthesised three reasons and three different pathways for evaluation:

- evaluation for *accountability* of the use or value of funding put into an intervention;
- evaluation for *development* to better understand and improve how change is brought about by an intervention;
- evaluation for *knowledge* to unravel often complex interactions within an intervention to assess, and build on, causal effects and added value.

A complicated theoretical base underpins each of these pathways, which will be looked at in subsequent chapters (see Chapters 4, 5 and 6). What is important at this stage is to recognise that evaluations have different drivers and different needs. An important practical difference is the likely rationale for an evaluation between mature and new (or recent) interventions. Where the intervention to be evaluated has been running for some time, possibly building on past programmes and activities, the evaluation is likely to be focusing on one, or more probably several, of, for example:

- demonstrating continuing value or worth of the funding or investment;
- evidencing if the initiative or specific parts of it can be improved or better focused to increase effectiveness (for example, targeting);
- assessing if there is scope for reorganisation or streamlining (usually for cost efficiencies);
- determining if, against changing circumstances, the actions are continuing to meet expectations.

For new or recent initiatives, including for pilot programmes, projects or activities, the reason for an evaluation being conducted is likely to be some combination of:

- making an initial assessment of whether the new idea is working: does it rise to the needs, outputs and outcomes expected of it?
- judging if it can be scaled up (for example, for a trial/pilot programme) and/or if it is cost-effective when it is rolled out (and what adaptations are needed for this);
- assessing if the intervention idea or process is transferable to other situations, and in what circumstances.

Evaluations are also likely to be carried out for the purposes of accountability and transparency of how resources were used. For some funding bodies (trusts, grant making foundations, charitable bodies) this may be the main goal for conducting an evaluation, so as to demonstrate that money was appropriately spent.

Evaluations being conducted in and around the public sector, and in particular in central government and its agencies, may have any of these needs but may also have some more specific administrative or policy-related reasons. Here, an evaluation may be required because it is:

- a *mandated evaluation*, perhaps part of a statutory or legislative commitment for regular or staged review of a policy, initiative or new regulation;
- subject to post-implementation reviews (PIRs in the UK) to assess the necessity or added value of, for example, a new regulation against a background of government seeking to streamline or reduce regulatory demands in society;
- part of a wider policy review process where evidence is needed to inform the focus and priorities for general or specified (for example, ring-fenced) government spending, or for improving unit cost and outcome efficiencies of government-funded systems;
- producing evidence that is needed to inform smarter and better government procurement of its services, and/or delivery effectiveness of outsourced or contracted activities.

This is not an exhaustive list of why an evaluation might be conducted, but it shows how even when the reason is 'because we have to", the circumstances and actual needs often differ. We shall go on to see how this fundamentally affects the choices later made on evaluation design and delivery (Chapter 3).

When to evaluate?

Practitioner's talk of *ex ante* and *ex post* evaluations – the first conducted before an intervention (perhaps to help with implementation or as a baseline to assess later achievements) the second after an intervention. Both describe when an evaluation is conducted, not when it should be. For this, a more useful distinction is between *formative* and *summative evaluation*. An early distinction between these types of evaluation came out of educational evaluation (Scriven, 1967) and they are now recognised as universal terms applying to evaluations, and their appropriate timing, so that:

- *Formative* evaluation provides an interim assessment(s) part the way through an intervention and usually to inform continuing improvement of actions.
- *Summative evaluation* provides a concluding assessment, perhaps at or close to the end of a pilot project so as to inform roll-out, or at the end of a funded period.

In some circumstances, the two can be combined with an evaluation providing staged (formative) findings and also an end or programme (summative) evaluation.

Looked at in this way, the 'right' timing of any evaluation will depend largely on the stage at which an intervention is made and decision makers' need of an evaluation. Experienced evaluators know that evaluation timing rarely has the luxury of being fully methods-led. In nearly all practical situations it is the other way around, with evaluators facing the challenges, set out in Chapter 3, of how to manage expectations of an evaluation to align with this.

Using the rest of this book

If evaluation is to be 'demystified' it needs straightforward explanation, practical guidance and a sufficient breadth of coverage to help readers get started. This chapter has set the scene.

The following chapters continue the practical emphasis on producing quality evaluations. For me, and for other policy-orientated evaluators, the quality of an evaluation is defined by the extent to which robust findings can be effectively utilised. Others have seen utilisation as the effective combination of choices made for fitness for purpose, relevance and credibility (Cousins and Leithwood, 1986). These are not standalone considerations; choices made for each will interact with options available for the others. However, for simplicity I have separated these out into what I think of as the three 'Cs' of effective evaluation:

- Compilation: building *fitness of purpose* through setting the right foundations, managing expectations, setting realistic objectives and handling ethical factors (Chapter 2)
- Composition: designing for *relevance* including scaling the evaluation, mixing primary and secondary evidence and proportionality of approach (Chapter 3)
- Conducting: providing for *credibility* through harnessing appropriate methodologies – looked at here through separate chapters on each of the main types of evaluation, namely, process, economic and impact evaluations (Chapters 4, 5 and 6).

The final part of the book looks at the analysis challenges and how the different roles in evaluation contribute to helping to make evidence useful and used (Chapter 7). It also touches on some of the emerging questions and issues likely to be facing those starting their evaluation journeys (Chapter 8). Along the way there are some real-world examples and a few handy tools are added as annexes.

This provides for a start, not an end. To help with further research on methods and options, a list of references is added and commended to readers.

2

COMPILATION: SETTING THE RIGHT FOUNDATIONS

- Different types of evaluation
- Choosing the evaluation focus – measurement vs understanding
- Tackling objective-setting and evaluation rationales
- Meeting needs and avoiding unrealistic expectations
- Addressing the moral dimension – evaluation ethics
- Resourcing, capability, independence and engagement in evaluation

Introduction

Compilation is the first of the three 'Cs' of evaluations. It is about the time and effort put into setting the foundations for an evaluation that is *fit for purpose*, and doing this before starting to consider methods and approach. Digging foundations may seem obvious, but the pressures on getting an evaluation started can mean that some of the compilation issues looked at in this chapter are too easily neglected. Paying full and urgent attention to compilation pays dividends downstream and avoids the risks of later delays or damage to credibility from starting off on the wrong foot.

Types of evaluation

The starting point in compilation is deciding just what sort of evaluation is to be conducted. The labels used to describe different types of evaluation do not always make it easy to make this choice, and the terminology can vary between disciplinary traditions, and even within them. In essence, the options can be reduced to:

- process evaluations
- economic evaluations
- impact evaluations.

Process evaluations: These focus on evaluating the mechanisms through which an intervention takes place, usually with a view to seeing how they could be improved. Process evaluations have attracted more variety in descriptions, sometimes being called *developmental* evaluations, or *management* evaluations. Whatever the label used, they share an emphasis on giving decision makers evidence of how (well) an intervention has been implemented or managed against expectations, how it operates, and how it produces what it does, rather than an understanding of what it has produced or its wider effects. With growing pressure on publicly funded or grant-funded services and initiatives, process evaluations are often a key evidence contribution to choices to be made on future priorities, streamlining or restructuring of activities.

Economic evaluations: A tightening public purse and pressure on margins and the 'bottom line' in many organisations mean that evaluations sometimes are focused wholly, or mainly, on measuring the costs of resource inputs or an intervention's value. Often this will need some comparative element to provide information about cost-effectiveness, usually in financial terms. Economic evaluations are not cost benefit assessments but often draw on similar measures (for example, value for money indexes) and methods of *monetising* inputs, outputs and outcomes.

Impact evaluations: Decision makers are often concerned with getting to grips with what comes out of an intervention, set against expectations of what was needed to address a particular problem or challenge. This type of evaluation is mostly concerned not with the activity or outputs of an intervention (as a process evaluation would be) but with measuring or estimating the *consequential change* that results from those activities/outputs. This is a challenge, since interventions often take place in complex environments where these impacts may have also been contributed to by influences from outside the intervention itself. Impact evaluation is consequently also concerned with looking at the *attribution* of impacts to what was done by the intervention itself.

Each of these types is looked at in more detail in Chapters 4, 5 and 6. For most practical purposes, evaluation needs are likely to fall into one of these broad categories. However, larger-scale, longitudinal or more complex evaluation of multifaceted interventions may combine one or more of these as a *pluralistic evaluation*, bringing together more than one evaluation type. An impact evaluation, for example, might include elements of process evaluation to evidence not only what changes took place, but also to understand what aspects or areas of the intervention were particularly effective in bringing those changes about.

A final type might be *meta-evaluation*. This is an evaluation of, or across, other evaluations, using evidence that has already been collected. This centres on a systematic review across these previous evaluations, aimed at critically reviewing and contrasting evidence to draw out common messages or learning. Meta-evaluation approaches are encouraged by some theorists as central to 'cumulation' of evidence to better understand or explain wider processes (Pawson and Tilley, 1997). However, such methods are not without their critics (St Leger et al, 1992), since there are challenges in bringing together suitable past evaluations that are close enough in focus, timing and approach to produce useful meta-analysis across these. Nevertheless, in some circumstances they provide a valuable tool.

Measurement vs understanding

Objective-setting is a key stage in compilation, but before evaluation compilers look at this, they need to consider if the type of evaluation they are planning is about 'measurement' or 'understanding'. It's helpful to look at this through the prism of the (mainly) academic debate about the nature of enquiry and examination, and in particular the differences between *positivism* and *interpretivism* (Figure 2.1).

The positivist approach is the one most closely associated with evaluators who need to focus on measurement and generalisability – that is, applying their findings to situations beyond the intervention itself. This developed from the early scientific roots of evaluation practice and meant that evaluators had an early and unquestioning focus on measuring outputs or outcomes, often using experimental methods (see Chapter 3). The emphasis was on quantitative measurement or

Figure 2.1: Evaluation relevance and the methodological field

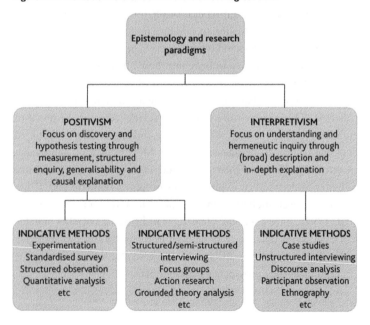

estimation to provide the necessary evidence to support decision makers. Qualitative data was seen as having no substantive role to play in producing empirical evidence, a view that can sometimes seem still deep-seated.

Measurement remains a vital underpinning of both economic and impact evaluations, and may also feature large in process evaluations. This provides a readily understood assessment of what an intervention has (or has not) produced. While there are risks in how to go about choosing and validating appropriate quantitative methods (see Chapter 7), these are relatively straightforward ways of assessing the relative 'success' of an intervention when reducing measurement to the difference between achievement and (any) previously set target or performance expectation.

In contrast, evaluation with understanding as its primary goal has roots in interpretivism, and it takes a rather different tack. It has taken a little longer for the value of this to be recognised within evaluation practice as both theorists and practitioners from the 1990s (and earlier in North America) started to question whether quantitative measurement was always enough to inform often complex decision-making needs. Understanding is concerned not with quantifying *how much* change has occurred, but with interpreting *how* change came about or the reasons *why* an intervention made a difference. Where this is important, evaluation needs a different emphasis and distinct methods.

For practically orientated evaluators, the alternatives of positivism or interpretivism are not mutually exclusive, although some research philosophers might have difficulty in accepting this. Evaluation theorists have also tended to side with one or the other. For example, early challenges to the science-based (first generation) approaches (Guba and Lincoln, 1989), and more recently the influential work by Pawson and Tilley on *realistic evaluation*, has given greater currency to interpretivist approaches (Pawson and Tilley, 1997). For me, measurement and understanding are not really competing alternatives, and 'how much' and 'how and why' can be combined in the same evaluation framework. The combination is often essential if decision makers are to have the breadth of evidence they need to make informed decisions.

Nonetheless, measurement and understanding reflect fundamentally different needs of evaluation. Recognising which (or what combinations) are needed is a key (early) part of evaluation compilation, and it will help determine later choices of evidence collection (and analytical) methods. Figure 2.2 summarises what focus is likely to apply to the different evaluation types.

Figure 2.2: Evaluation types and information needs

Type of evaluation	Measurement: *how much*	Understanding: *how* and *why*	Measurement + understanding combined
Process evaluation	√		√
Economic evaluation	√		
Impact evaluation	√	√	√
Pluralistic evaluation	√	√	√

Measurement vs understanding is important for one other reason. Where measurement is the sole or main focus for the evaluation, what is being measured can be assessed comparatively against other similar interventions or activity, or benchmarked (for example, by looking at what happened pre-intervention or in past practice). This is not so easy where the focus is on understanding. Benchmarking for *how* and *why* is likely to need a clear and explicit set of assumptions about how the intervention will work or make a difference. Evaluators refer to this as a *theory of change*, an important focus for compilation of evaluation, which has grown from a combination of the work of evaluation theorists (Guba and Lincoln, 1989; Chen, 1990; Pawson and Tilley, 1997; and notably from Weiss, 1997) and more practical perspectives.

Ideas about evaluation and theory of change stemmed from looking at how *programme theory* could apply a structure for evaluating specific interventions. The 'theory' part of it is not about the evaluation itself but about the why and wherefore of the intervention to be evaluated. A clear and explicit programme theory helps shape the focus of the evaluation. Chen saw this consisting of two separate but interrelated parts: *normative theory* and *causative theory* (Chen, 1990):

- Normative theory sets out how the programme (intervention) is expected to operate and can be used to provide evaluation evidence for process improvements.
- Causative theory sets out how different parts of an intervention are expected to work together to produce change, and this can be used to identify unintended as well as intended consequences in an impact evaluation.

Other approaches are also possible, and one review of applications of programme theory (in community development initiatives) suggested that their quality was determined by plausibility, feasibility and testability (Kubisch, 1997). These remain very useful ways of assessing the quality of a theory and change, and its practicability, with the testability aspect underpinning evaluation potential.

Much more could be said about programme theory and theory of change, and there is no shortage of guidance on how to construct such a tool for developing solutions to complex social problems (for example, Harris et al, 2012). For now, all we need to know is that this approach underpins much government and other policy and practice in building business cases for interventions, and is often expected of voluntary, community and other organisations seeking public, trust or charitable project funding. These can be quite complex documents, but these days are often condensed into simplified *logic chains* (see Figure 2.3) which summarise the theory of change for an intervention and the expectations of it.

Figure 2.3: A logic chain

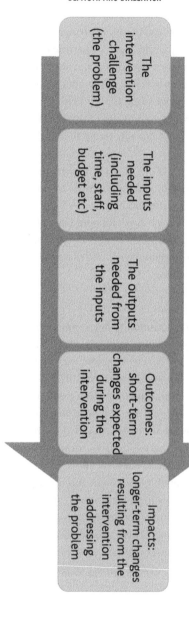

The intervention challenge (the problem)

The inputs needed (including time, staff, budget etc)

The outputs needed from the inputs

Outcomes: short-term changes expected during the intervention

Impacts: longer-term changes resulting from the intervention addressing the problem

Source: Adapted from HM Treasury, 2011

Logic chains (some call them logic charts or logic frames) will set out the essence of the intervention. They may be set out in all sorts of different ways, although a simple tabular form (as illustrated by Example 1) is often best. Used in this way they provide for:

- a clear, concise (and accepted) statement of the **challenge** (or problem or issue) that an intervention is expected to tackle;
- the **inputs** needed to put the intervention in place and make it work (this may also include a separate statement of constituent activities but I usually find inputs and activities combined provide for a simpler format);
- the **outputs** expected to be delivered as a result of the intervention doing what it is intended to do;
- the **outcomes and impacts** expected to result from the inputs and outputs – with a distinction made between what consequential changes can be expected in the short term (for example, from a beneficiary participating in the intervention) and in the longer term (for example, behavioural changes which may take some time to come about).

Logic charts come in various shapes and sizes and are always customised to the particular intervention. Typically they are set out in chart or tabular form, as with the simple example in Example 1 below.

Example 1: A logic chart for a sector skills initiative

Problems to address	Inputs	Outputs	Outcomes (<2 years)	Impacts (3–5 years)
There is a skills gap in the industry's ability to apply lean and modern manufacturing techniques to [sector] processes	• Direct engagement of leaders/executive managers from lead manufacturers (x6) • Cascade commitment from HR, functional mid and technical staff from lead manufacturers • Involvement of leaders, managers and technical staff from supply chain (>50) • Marketing and skills diagnostic expertise • Programme budget	• A new and consistent method for clients and contractors to engage with the supply chain on skills devlopment • A tool to diagnose organisation skills gap • Agreed audit-based sector need analysis for supply and demand gaps, timeframe and priorities • Develop cross-sector benchmark using audit aggregates benchmark • 250 businesses engaged in new learning	• Employees in >50 existing offsite suppliers gain improved skills filling defined gaps • New skills supply capacity • Engaged companies report 50+% fall in skills gaps and 25+% fall in recruitment difficulty • Engaged companies report +25% fall in absence • Greater collaboration across the supply chain	Tackling the five identified problems will lead to impacts at an industry and company level – within 5 years from start. **Industry level** The industry will be able to meet the strategic objectives set out in the UK [sector] strategy: • Min 15% rise in productivity • 33% cost reductions • 50% faster [sector] • 50% less carbon **Company level** Those companies with these new skills will benefit from: • aggregate +5% rise market share in the UK • ability to access international markets. This is turn will lead to increased employment and gross value added for those businesses with the new skills
There is no consistent way to diagnose the skills gap and benchmark best practice	• Skills diagnosis and delivery expertise across acknowledged areas of skills deficiencies • IT and financial resources	• Develop and test a cross-sector skills diagnostic framework tool (x1) for self-administration	• Companies understand their skills requirements • Enhanced skills for 2,000+ employee's in first 12 months; +500 next 2 years	

Problems to address	Inputs	Outputs	Outcomes (<2 years)	Impacts (3–5 years)
There is a need for easily accessible industry standard offsite learning materials	• Skills expertise across a number of acknowledged areas of skills deficiencies • IT and financial resources	• Build and test a content-rich 'gap' based web learning platform (x 1) • Develop and test 10 x e-learning units • 1 x resource library • 2,500 first-year users	• Companies report 50%+ fall in supply problems for identified skills needs, 75%+ rise in reported skills supply responsiveness, 50%+ rise in skills supply flexibility	
Lack of collaboration for solutions and capacity to deliver across the value chain	• Involvement of leaders/managers in value chain • Facilitation expertise and budget	• Establish Employers Leadership Group	• Improved collaboration reported by 75%+ engaged companies	
Need to stimulate evidence-based (gap) demand from lead manufacturers and contractors	• Consultation and marketing plans • Involvement of leaders, managers and technical staff from supply chain, design teams, engineering • Marketing, technical and IT expertise and budget	• Develop subsector generic training solutions for lead manufacturers and contractors (supply chain) • 3 x dedicated learning zones in the online module for clients, designers and contractors	• Increased demand for offsite solutions in at least 50+% of engaged companies	

By setting out clear expectations of the 'hows' and 'whys' of an intervention, logic charts provide a theory of change benchmark against which an evaluation can focus on *understanding*. Their value, however, applies to any intervention to be evaluated, whether the focus is to be on measurement or understanding, since they set out the rationale for an intervention and what is expected of it, including quantified activities, targets and (some) outcomes. This becomes a foundation of theory-based approaches to evaluation (Treasury Board of Canada Secretariat, 2012) and is key to the next step in compilation: setting evaluation objectives.

Objective-setting and evaluation rationales

Evaluations are not bought or chosen off-the-peg; they do not follow a standard emphasis or pattern. The focus of each will vary with the context of what is to be evaluated (and decision-makers' needs of it), and so too will the objectives set for the evaluators. Setting the 'right' evaluation objectives is perhaps the most critical part of the compilation stage yet paying enough attention to it is easily neglected. Too often one comes across evaluation specifications which are vague, imprecise and not well-fitted to the intervention being evaluated. As Example 2 shows, it is not uncommon to find objectives set out which are not objectives at all.

Example 2: How not to set evaluation goals

A very large UK heritage organisation running a pilot programme to reshape its activities for schools and colleges asked for evaluators to conduct a process and impact evaluation of its planned new education programme. It specified:

> The evaluation goal is to assess the effectiveness and effects of the pilot and lessons learned for [the rollout of the organisation's new education programme] ... with the objectives of analysing management information, conducting major stakeholder interviews, a survey of providers participating in the pilot, and providing a small number of provider case studies and reporting with recommendations to ...

While the general goal (if a little vague) is clear, the 'objectives' say little about what decisions the pilot evaluation is expected to inform and nothing on what evidence is needed and why. Only the last – reporting and recommendations – could be said to be a clear objective; the rest are statements of method with no apparent rationale for why they are proposed. This organisation is not alone among those procuring evaluations, in jumping into statements about methods without being clear about what difference the evaluation itself is expected to make, to what precise policy or programme intervention, for what reasons or expectations or what the broad evidence needs will be to support this.

The starting point for objective-setting is the overall rationale for the evaluation: why it is being conducted? Here, if the intervention has a programme theory or logic chain, it can help greatly with setting out the rationale and cascading this to more specific appropriate objectives. It can also help when asking others (top managers, funders, stakeholders, peers, etc.) for comments on draft objectives, because it provides a common reference point as to why an intervention is being conducted and what is expected to be involved.

Although it is a well-worn convention, evaluations, like other project-based activity, will be focused most effectively where objectives are S-M-A-R-T. There are various connotations of 'SMART' but for those setting (or critically reviewing) evaluation goals, Figure 2.4 summarises what is most likely to be involved.

Figure 2.4: Using the SMART framework to set evaluation objectives

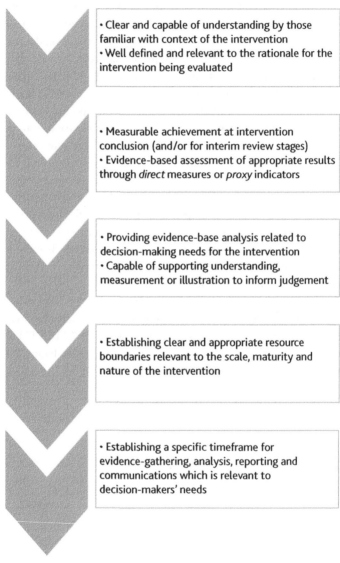

• Clear and capable of understanding by those familiar with context of the intervention
• Well defined and relevant to the rationale for the intervention being evaluated

• Measurable achievement at intervention conclusion (and/or for interim review stages)
• Evidence-based assessment of appropriate results through *direct* measures or *proxy* indicators

• Providing evidence-base analysis related to decision-making needs for the intervention
• Capable of supporting understanding, measurement or illustration to inform judgement

• Establishing clear and appropriate resource boundaries relevant to the scale, maturity and nature of the intervention

• Establishing a specific timeframe for evidence-gathering, analysis, reporting and communications which is relevant to decision-makers' needs

Source: Author's teaching materials (*Advanced Evaluation*, Social Research Association)

Using the SMART yardstick might have seen the heritage organisation in Example 2 produce a clearer initial aim and objectives for the evaluation. Example 3 shows how these might have looked.

Example 3: SMART evaluation goals

The large UK heritage organisation (Example 2) might have reset its evaluation goals as:

The evaluation goal is to assess the effectiveness, benefits and early outcomes of the educational pilot programme against [the organisation's] new educational development goals and to set out implications for the extension of the pilot programme nationally for the mutual benefit of [the organisation] and educational partners. More specific objectives for the evaluation will be to:

a) assess against the pilot programme's targets the achieved scale and quality of educational partners' engagement across the constituent activities of the pilot;

b) review and explain variations in the quality of engagement for different educational partners;

c) assess the early achieved outcomes for educational partners (and the contribution of the pilot) including for students' learning experiences and educational outcomes;

d) review better practice among education partners in engaging effectively with the pilot activities;

e) provide a full report of the evaluation with evidence-based recommendations for improvement and national rollout.

If the 'right' objectives are not set for an evaluation, decision makers are not likely to get (all) the evidence they need to make judgements about an intervention. The challenge for evaluators is determining just what is 'right' for each evaluation. This will not just be a technical assessment of what is possible for that specific intervention; it is likely to need to draw on different perspectives about what the evaluation objectives are meant to mean and the intended use. For those involved at the front end of an evaluation, setting the right evaluation objectives is consequently often an iterative process, engaging with those making decisions or judgements about what is useful, and sometimes with other stakeholders. The 'SMART' framework is a simple and practical tool that can help with this.

Avoiding unrealistic expectations

As a peer reviewer of governmental and other evaluations for government departments and other agencies, I have seen more evaluations that have been compromised by unrealistic expectations that had gone unchallenged, than by inappropriate design or analysis choices. Too often the objectives facing evaluators are often not 'SMART' (or smart-enough) and this can result in muddled or misleading expectations of what the evaluation can do.

Unrealistic expectations of evaluations are surprisingly commonplace. Objective-setting may lack a programme rationale, or it may be rushed or limited by a narrow perspective of what is needed. Expectations may be shaped in isolation from its users, with those most likely to be using the evaluation findings not consulted on its scope or focus. Those setting objectives may just be inexperienced in doing so. Whatever the cause, evaluation and evaluators need to be acutely aware of the likelihood and risks of unrealistic expectations. Typically this may come from one or more of:

- lack of an underpinning rationale for what (and why) the evaluation is being conducted;
- little (or no) coherence between the evaluation objectives and any intervention rationale that has been formulated;
- a defined scope for an evaluation that is ill-fitted to what is needed in terms of evidence collection or decision-making needs
- inadequate resources allowed for the evaluation objectives/scope
- lack of clarity on how the evaluation findings will be used (and/ or who the users are)
- imprecisely specified objectives for the evaluation (not SMART).

Any one of these presents a real risk of a car crash in the subsequent use of the evaluation findings.

While it is best to set realistic expectations before choices are made on types of evaluation or their designs, this is too often not the situation facing someone tasked with specifying or carrying out an evaluation. The solution is not to accept at face value any inherited objectives or expectations and to critically review any that are handed down. Figure 2.5 sets out a valuable tool for doing that: the **R**oles **O**utcomes **T**iming **U**sers **R**esources (ROTUR) framework.

Figure 2.5: The ROTUR framework for managing expectations

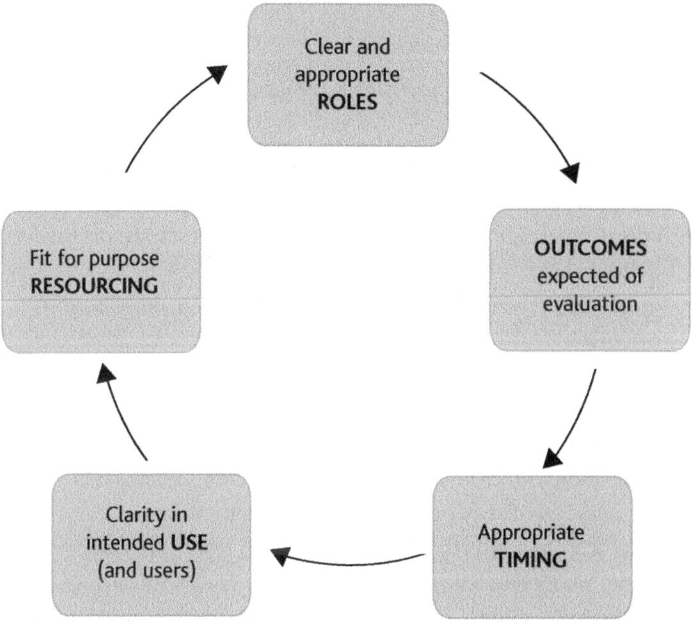

Source: Author's teaching materials (*Advanced Evaluation*, Social Research Association).

The ROTUR framework can be used as drafting tool by those setting evaluation goals and expectations, or to help with critical appraisal by those asked to take an evaluation forward. It is a guide that can be used in widely different evaluation circumstances, and Annex A provides this in more detail to show how the framework approach can be used in practice.

Using ROTUR, or another way to critically review objectives and expectations, helps in identifying inconsistencies or impracticalities, pointing out potential pitfalls before they become problems. This provides a basis for adjusting unrealistic objectives or general expectations either pre-procurement (by those specifying the evaluation) or post-procurement and before contracting (by project managers or evaluators themselves). Typically this will involve one or more of:

- tightening the precise wording or meaning of specific requirements;
- adding specific measurement goals or aspirations for understanding the intervention;
- adjusting timeframes (for example, interim, draft or final deliverables);
- modifying terminology to make the objectives more action-orientated.

Aims or objectives can be adjusted directly with(in) the client organisations, or through discussion in project or steering groups for the evaluation. Alternatively, for external evaluators, contractual caveats can be added to clarify precise needs and expectations.

Even if is too late to change objectives and expectations (for example, post contracting) a *better later than never* critical review by the evaluator(s) still has a role to play. This can identify any confusion or lack of 'SMART-ness' and provide for a discussion (and some documentation) that sharpens expectations of what is being asked for and how it will be used. Typically this could be tackled at inception stage or shortly after, and before design choices are made for evaluations to provide for greater realism in how evaluation evidence can be used.

Paradoxically, those new to evaluation, or inexperienced, may be the most reluctant to take these steps to manage expectations. They may lack the confidence to recognise unrealistic expectations, or the skills and working relationships to challenge them with specifiers or users. They may be subject to real or imagined pressure to 'get on with it', 'make the best of it', or 'avoid rocking the boat'. They need to remember that while challenging unrealistic expectations may delay an evaluation start, or risk putting the evaluator in a difficult position early in the process, the costs of not doing so – namely, unmet expectations or inappropriate evidence or analysis to meet users' needs – are potentially much greater.

The moral dimension

The largest professional body of evaluators, the American Evaluation Association, among others, has set out a moral dimension role in the compilation (and conduct) of evaluations so that:

> Evaluators should abide by current professional ethics, standards, and regulations regarding risks, harms, and burdens that might befall those participating in the evaluation; regarding informed consent for participation in evaluation; and regarding informing participants and clients about the scope and limits of confidentiality. (AEA, 2004, D2)

Putting this (and other) guidance into practice is a recurrent challenge for evaluators, and nearly 20 years ago Carol Weiss, an architect of the wider American Evaluation Association (AEA) principles, observed:

> Evaluation has an obligation to pay even more attention to ethical questions than most other kinds of social science research. (Weiss, 1998a, p 92)

This obligation stems from the very nature of evaluation and what it is about. It will often mean dealing with people (directly or indirectly) who are participants or beneficiaries in an intervention, who may be from disadvantaged, incapacitated or vulnerable groups, and for whom the findings of an evaluation may have real consequences. So the ethical dimension looms large in evaluation principles and practice, with a moral obligation on evaluators in making and delivering design choices. Fortunately for such sensitive issues, there is an extensive literature dealing with ethics in evaluation, and while this adopts different philosophical standpoints, four broad ethical principles can be drawn from it:

- avoiding harm in the collection of evidence, data storage and communication;
- providing for fairness in evidence gathering and interpretation,
- ensuring independence across the evaluation process;
- providing for effective and appropriate communication of findings (and implications).

Guidance in the professional and other codes of practice, such as that from the AEA, helps to unpick these elements and to go beyond evidence-gathering issues (for example, informed consent) to look at the implications for individual evaluation designs and circumstances. As set out in parallel guidance from the UK Evaluation Society (UKES), there are three broad constituencies for the moral dimension:

- participants and others supplying evidence to support an evaluation;
- evaluation practitioners and especially those gathering and analysing that evidence;
- evaluation sponsors and stakeholders directly involved in using evaluation findings.

Ethical considerations for participants

Evaluation design needs to take robust steps to ensure that those volunteering to take part should not be adversely affected by the evaluation process. Particular issues to take into account include:

- avoidance of harm (for example, through risk assessment and use of appropriate countermeasures to eliminate or minimise risk);
- voluntary participation with clearly signposted rights of withdrawal (from specific areas of questioning or from participation altogether);
- action in evidence gathering to minimise participant duress and embarrassment;
- action to ensure fairness and equity in contributor selection and support;
- a clearly expressed guarantee of the agreed level of anonymity and/or confidentiality;
- systems and procedures to optimise safety and security, including security of data.

Others might be relevant to particular circumstances. Underpinning each of these is the need for informed consent, where participants will be informed (usually in writing) of:

- the evaluation origins, purpose, and funding source;
- the aims, procedures, benefits and alternatives to participation;
- any 'risks' from participation, countermeasures (for example, security of transcripts or data);
- access (where appropriate) to harm mitigation support for contributors;
- the need for formal consent (often signed) to participation.

Some evidence gathering may be with potential participants who may lack the capacity to provide informed consent (eg young people, adults with learning disabilities) and where provision needs to be made for proxies or helpers to provide for safeguards in informed consent.

Ethical considerations for practitioners

Ethical issues also affect the evaluators themselves, and in particular those collecting the evidence and analysing it. Here, evaluation design and delivery needs to ensure:

- practitioners are free from any relevant (undeclared) potential conflicts of interest;
- appropriate steps are taken to provide evaluator safety and protection in the field;
- practitioners follow professional standards and requirements and ensure high standards of integrity and honesty through the evaluation process;
- evidence and data gathered are supported with appropriate security for data protection, storage and transmission;
- practitioners at all stages are free from any coercion, including from the coverage of evidence, representation of findings or exclusion of evidence.

Shaw has suggested that for evaluations to be effective and credible, evidence gathering and interpretation needs *to be seen to be* just, fair and independent (Shaw, 1999). The ethical conduct of evaluators is central to ensuring that no uncertainties about conflicts of interest, integrity or coercion can produce doubts about, or a diversion from, the findings of the evaluation when it is concluded.

Ethical considerations and sponsors

Evaluations also have ethical responsibilities to those funding the evaluation, or requiring it to be carried out, which include:

- ensuring effective alignment of (sponsor) expectations and needs with the evaluation design and delivery;
- demonstrable quality in evidence gathering, collation and analysis;

- reliable representation of evidence, including justification for positive and negative findings;
- full disclosure of analytical limits and limitations, including in the reporting process;
- application and practicability in establishing recommendations from evidence;
- assurance of ethical compliance across the evaluation.

Last, but not least, evaluators have a responsibility to sponsors for effective communication of evidence. I would contend that this does not end with reporting. Evaluators have a responsibility to help communicate the findings and to assist in exploring implications. Not all sponsors will welcome such involvement. In some, the organisational culture may resist those from outside and therefore the idea of evaluators playing a more direct role in communicating evidence and its implications. Yet experience shows that those taking decisions guided by the evaluation evidence may not have thoroughly familiarised themselves with the findings, its limits and caveats (for example, on generalisability). Evaluators will be closest to the evidence (and its strengths and weaknesses) and best placed to guide them, albeit with their role as independent evaluators falling short of direct involvement in the decision-making process. These are complex and sensitive issues and are returned to in Chapter 7.

So, the moral dimension of evaluation is important but is rarely straightforward or easy. This introduction may help unpick some of the elements but each evaluator will need to find out if there are particular codes, principles or practices they must comply with in specific instances; and if not, which principles they should follow for guidance. The AEA Guiding Principles have passed the test of time but others may also be well suited to different evaluation contexts. For those looking for more general guidance on the moral dimension, a good starting point is the high-level principles set out in the *New Brunswick Declaration on Research Ethics, Integrity and Governance* (New Brunswick Declaration, 2013), and to which the UK's Social Research Association and numerous professional and public bodies are signatories.

Resourcing, capability and independence

A recurrent question that faces decision makers is whether an evaluation is best done internally or externally. The choice is not quite as stark as it may seem, however, and there are likely to be four main options:

- in-house evaluation
- self-evaluation
- external (commissioned) evaluation
- hybrid resourcing

There is no rule by which to determine which approach is best for a particular situation, but taking account of the different benefits, and also limitations, makes the choice easier.

In-house evaluation

This will involve the sponsoring or funding body carrying out the evaluation internally, typically using their own staff, and will probably be:

- cheaper (although arguably staff costs will be hidden and will probably come from an internal budget);
- more likely to be 'owned' within the organisation since it is being conducted by known staff with an internal track record;
- less likely to suffer data-access constraints, since much of what is needed for evidence gathering (or access to participants) is likely to be accessible in-house;
- making use of 'contextual knowledge', with the evaluator likely to be close to the intervention, its delivery and policy context;
- quicker, providing for a typically faster start than externally commissioned evaluations (this may be especially important for very intensive evaluations).

At the same time, there are drawbacks. The staff undertaking the evaluation may not always be 'hand-picked' for their knowledge and evaluation experience, risking quality and authoritativeness. Because it is reliant on available staff, there are risks other resourcing priorities may intervene, leading to the evaluation slipping down the internal priorities list. But the most common drawback is simply how it will be perceived; an in-house evaluation, however robustly it is designed and analysed, is not likely to be seen as independent.

Self-evaluation

In resource-constrained environments, with subcontracting of services and service innovations more commonplace, grant making and some public bodies may stipulate that it is for the contractor to conduct their own evaluation. Self-evaluation may be a useful option, especially for very small-scale requirements, and can draw on substantial practitioner expertise within interventions. This type of evaluation will have many of the same benefits, and drawbacks, as an in-house evaluation, although it is even more likely that the staff tasked with conducting such an evaluation will lack the necessary skills or experience. Even more than an in-house evaluation, a self-evaluation will also face the risk that findings will not be seen as authoritative and those that are difficult for users to embrace will be dismissed simply with: "Well, they would say that wouldn't they."

External evaluation

External evaluations will be commissioned by the direct funding body (or perhaps by subcontractors) from outside, nonaligned evaluators, perhaps consultants, academics or independent research groups. Unless evaluations are very small-scale, these will almost always require some form of structured procurement and commissioning, which will take time. However, they have the benefit of being:

- recognisably independent – professional evaluators, with no conflicts of interest (usually screened out in procurement), will not be seen as 'having an axe to grind';
- 'expert' (if well selected) and able to make use of specialist expertise/techniques that may not be known to less experienced (in-house) staff or practitioners;
- able to draws on wider comparative knowledge, perhaps about similar policy initiatives or interventions that may be of additional value to the evaluation analysis;
- likely to be taken more seriously than staff conducting an in-house or self-evaluation.

These are powerful and often persuasive benefits, but external evaluations will inevitably need a budget and they will cost (a lot) more. As 'external' to the intervention, they may also encounter data access constraints such as data protection limitations on personalised data, and they may be regarded with suspicion by project staff ('not one of us'). They are also likely to need a longer timetable, to allow for the delays involved in procurement and start-up – delays that might add 8–10 weeks or more to an evaluation timetable.

Engagement in effective evaluation

Engagement in evaluation tends to be seen as an issue in delivery, in engaging effectively with those providing access to data or participants, or with participants themselves to help build credibility. This is important, but engagement is just as important before and after evidence gathering in helping to build fitness for purpose and confidence in the findings (an issue returned to in Chapter 8). Here, engagement goes beyond commissioning bodies, perhaps to include provider perspectives and those of other stakeholders if problems or challenges to the evaluation are anticipated.

Not all stakeholders will be willing collaborators; evaluations present challenges to those with a stake in the outcome of findings and analysis, and some will be cautious, even adversarial. The easy path will be to avoid early difficulty but this has a price and too often leads to more acute problems downstream. Such problems with stakeholders could have been raised and resolved more easily at this compilation stage.

The composition of project steering groups for larger-scale evaluations may take this into account, but commissioning bodies themselves may be cautious about involving doubters among members. Where this is the case, and where it can be negotiated, evaluators are well advised to be proactive in opening other channels for engagement. If for no other reason, evaluator integrity and fairness will also mean that an independent analysis needs to take account of all viewpoints, even those less well-disposed either to the evaluation or what is being evaluated. Paradoxically, this more open approach to engagement can pay dividends downstream if unforeseen problems occur. It may also deliver benefits towards the end of the evaluation in reducing some stakeholders' suspicions about the evaluation process, its independence and its credibility. Time spent on early engagement is usually time very well spent.

3

COMPOSITION: DESIGNING FOR NEEDS

- Scaling and scope: the differences between small 'n' and 'large 'n' evaluation
- Deciding on 'core' information needs and sourcing available secondary evidence
- Identifying evidence gaps and using primary evidence collection to fill these
- Using hybrid evaluation designs to build robustness and triangulate sources
- Proportionality and cost-effectiveness in evaluation designs
- Taking early account of data protection and data security needs
- Anticipating the analysis requirements and implications.

Introduction

With the foundations set, attention turns from compilation to composition. This is where evaluators start to get to grips with the wider design issues that come ahead of the specific choices to be made about methodology. Attention to detail at this compilation stage is important and makes the difference between underpinning or undermining subsequent choices on what evidence to collect, where and how to collect it, and how to interpret it – issues returned to separately for process, economic and impact evaluation in Chapters 4, 5 and 6.

Scaling and scope

The starting point in composition is to consider the likely scale of the evaluation, building on judgements already made in compilation (Chapter 2). Scale is much more than an issue of 'how big for the budget?', and, ideally, decisions on scale should lead decisions on budget and not vice versa. In tackling scale, evaluators make a distinction between:

- small 'n' evaluation
- large 'n' evaluation

Here, 'small' and 'large' are relative to the nature of the intervention and its maturity, and 'n' relates to the overall size and scope of participation in what is being evaluated. A small 'n' evaluation, for example, might look at a trial of a new online application or assessment process for a particular beneficiary group. The trial might be carried out over a short period, perhaps in one city and with only a handful of applicants, with the evaluation aimed at early evidence of how well the new online system is working compared to an existing advisor and office-based system. As with most small 'n' evaluations, this might be expected to produce findings often quite speedily, looking at individuals' experiences in some depth, perhaps by covering all or most of the few trial participants. This same intervention may later need a large 'n' evaluation when lessons have been learned from the trial, changes have been made and the new process has been rolled out nationally to replace or run alongside the 'old' system.

Small 'n' approaches are often associated with social contexts and situations that rely heavily on use of readily available and embedded evidence for an intervention, often partnering evaluators with delivery organisations (Hall and Hall, 2004). They remain bound by the same needs for ensuring fitness for purpose, relevance and credibility as large 'n' evaluations, and are not simply a substitute where budgets or timeframes are constrained. However, small 'n' evaluations are quite different in their scope and the small size of what is being evaluated means they are constrained to address these issues in different ways. In particular, small 'n' evaluations usually place great weight on exploring existing monitoring evidence, typically alongside small-scale qualitative inputs, which are often in the form of case studies. The aim is to build up an in-depth assessment based on weight of evidence, strength of argument, and by establishing the absence of other plausible explanations for outcomes and effects.

Large 'n' evaluations, in contrast, have much greater methodological choice open to them. This brings with it responsibilities, not only in choosing the most appropriate methods and applications, but also to demonstrate that the evidence generated is credible, robust and statistically valid – issues returned to in Chapter 7.

Information needs and sourcing: secondary analysis

Whatever the most appropriate scale of the evaluation, designing for needs will require a constructively critical, and early, look at what information is needed for meeting the objectives and applying subsequent findings. This is likely to involve a mix of:

- secondary evidence – that which can be brought to hand readily from 'desk research' of existing sources (including past research and evaluation);
- primary evidence to fill information needs and gaps that cannot be met by secondary evidence; this involves new evidence gathering.

For the evaluator, juggling this mix of secondary and primary evidence may be the first point where they feel they are on solid ground, making design choices with methods and sources that may be familiar and where they are confident of what is necessary and/or possible. Not all evaluations use both secondary and primary sources, and much depends on the information needs and potential coming out of the objectives or evaluation (research) questions stemming from them. In addition, the evidence gathering context and limitations (including the ethical considerations looked at in compilation, Chapter 2) are important. Primary evidence is looked at below but a sound starting point for any evaluation is using information that is to hand or can be readily accessed.

Using secondary evidence is about more than keeping costs down, although this remains an important driver in today's resource-constrained environment. It is important because it makes best use of what is already available and does not waste resources on capturing evidence (from primary sources) that has already been collected by others. More specifically:

- It may provide useful early evidence to refine assumptions about information needs (and availability) or to develop subsequent evaluation (new evidence gathering) tools.
- It may be able to provide a baseline from which to measure *distance travelled* – for example, what added outputs have been generated or what participant changes or improvements have taken place within the intervention.
- It might be able to provide for a comparative dimension – drawing on other research or evaluation evidence to determine how effective other similar interventions (or initiatives addressing similar challenges and problems) have been.
- It can be crucial where evaluations are particularly intensive and where the time may not be available for putting in place new (primary) evidence gathering arrangements.

Of course, not all of the data readily to hand will be appropriate; on occasions little or none of it may be of value. The evaluator will need do draw on their critical faculties and knowledge of the nature of the intervention being evaluated, to identify what evidence is available through clients, stakeholders, providers and perhaps participants, but also to assess its relevance (what it covers and when) and utility (how it was collected, its coverage and quality). This data may have been collected and collated by others, often for different purposes, so may not fit the evaluation's needs. It is the evaluator's responsibility to make the necessary judgements about any limitations.

Secondary sources cover both quantitative and qualitative evidence and might include, for example, information from legacy data (for example, past practice) programme (intervention) monitoring data, participant or incident records, and management information (from providers and/or partner organisations). Although it may be stretching the conventional definition of 'secondary' sources, available national (official) or non-official statistics also provide valuable contextual information and may even support meta-analysis where a range of data sources can be tapped. A lot can often be achieved from harnessing secondary sources, especially in data-rich situations, as with the burgeoning of digital technology, online and technology embedded monitoring, which is becoming more common. Example 4 shows an example of an award-winning community project which relied wholly on available evidence sources.

Example 4: An impact evaluation using secondary sources

Project Bernie started as a small-scale pilot project in a partnership between local public services in South Wales in the UK. It aimed to tackle a persistent community safety and environmental problem of deliberate grassfire setting in urban fringes, causing great damage to local amenity, wildlife and habitat, with many hundreds of callouts of the emergency services each year. A community-based social marketing, alternative activity and branded education intervention was planned, but limited resources and the 'risk' period for fire-setting required this to be condensed to a single six-week period during the school summer vacation. Preceded by university research to understand social causes, the pilot needed to be evaluated for its impact and added value in just a 10-week period, and could use only secondary evidence.

Using a matched-comparator area method, both historic and current data were collected from incident records (South Wales Fire and Rescue Service), damage, offending and other monitoring data (police and local authorities) and analysed against monitoring information collected 'in pilot'. Contrasting data for the Project Bernie pilot area (Tonypandy in the South Wales Valleys) with a closely matched comparator area (Aberdare), the evaluation across multiple indicators from these data sources showed a large net reduction (43%) in deliberate grass-fire setting in the pilot area, and also net impact spinoffs across a range of measures of (reduced) antisocial behaviour. Using this evidence, South Wales Fire and Rescue Service secured three-year funding to roll out (and further evaluate) the intervention in other areas.

Although not relevant to Project Bernie, past research or literature may also be valuable in scene-setting or providing comparative evidence (of practice, outcomes and influences identified elsewhere). Most evaluations will have neither the time nor resources to use formal systematic review methods to assess past knowledge, and methods such as rapid evidence review are more likely to be better fitted to evaluation circumstances.

Most readers will be familiar with secondary sources and analysis from research methods training at university or college and perhaps subsequent research experience. However, they should be cautious about relying wholly on sources they know or analytical methods with which they are familiar from particular disciplinary contexts; use of secondary (and primary) sources may mean operating outside a methodological comfort zone. Fortunately, there is also no shortage of guidance on how to apply such methods (see, for example, the early text of Stewart and Kamins, 1993).

Primary evidence and gap analysis

It is unlikely (although certainly not impossible, as the Project Bernie example shows) that all the information needs of an evaluation will be delivered by secondary sources and analysis). Primary sources are used to fill the gaps between what is appropriate and available and what is needed to provide a sufficient evidence base to address the evaluation objectives. For the evaluator, the options for using primary evidence sources will greatly exceed the potential to exploit them within a specific evaluation and hard choices need to be made about what primary evidence is needed and can be viably (and validly) collected.

The expectations of the evaluation (and often the specification itself) may already have made some assumptions. Calls for participant surveys or interviews, stakeholder review, or 'best practice' case studies, may have more to do with aspirations than sound methodological judgement, but they provide a starting point. A more systematic basis for assessing where primary evidence is needed is to use a 'gap analysis' approach, perhaps based on the model example in Figure 3.1 below.

This is a tried and tested approach to defining where primary evidence gathering is needed, consistent with the aspirations and needs of the evaluation users. Its success, however, lies in the scoping of the initial research questions (step 1), the quality and comprehensiveness of the mapping (steps 3 and 4) as well as the value judgements made about what is 'crucial' and what is 'viable' (steps 6 and 7).

Overlaying all this is also the quality of engagement that can be brought to bear on testing and enhancing the proposals (steps 2 and 8). Testing is important not just in sharpening the gap analysis but, in due course, in providing users with enough information about what is being collected (and how) to judge the validity of subsequent conclusions and recommendations.

Just as with secondary sources, most readers will be familiar with the range of qualitative and quantitative methods that can be employed to fill crucial gaps and these are not repeated here. However, readers may need to be cautious about what may be called disciplinary prejudice for or against particular methods. Different disciplines, or different teaching traditions, often favour particular evidence-gathering methods which are better suited to the subject (and subject matter) of that discipline. Evaluators (even if they describe themselves as multidisciplinary) will be drawn from one of those *home* disciplines and may be naturally suspicious of some methods and favour (or have less experience of) others that are more commonplace in other disciplinary traditions. In framing a gap analysis for primary evidence gathering, evaluators need to be open-minded about different possibilities and choosing what

Figure 3.1: A model approach to identifying and filling primary evidence needs for an evaluation

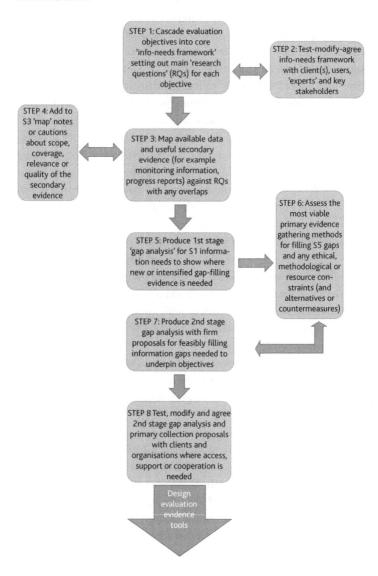

best fits the needs. A crucial part of making those choices is ensuring that whatever gap-filling methods are chosen, they are *proportionate* to the circumstances and requirements of the evaluation, a vital issue that we will return to shortly.

Hybrid designs and their use

The composition stage of an evaluation is not about making choices *between* collecting primary or secondary evidence and analytical methods, or whether the orientation is to be quantitative or qualitative; nor is it about whether the findings are to be (statistically) representative or indicative. Some evaluation designs may legitimately be wholly one or the other of these (what is called a *pure* or *coherent* design) but the choices are more often *across* them, using differently focused methods in combination. We refer to these simply as hybrid or mixed mode designs, and they come in as many different shapes and sizes as the subjects of evaluations themselves.

To some readers, *hybrid* may have connotations of impure, compromised or second best designs. This is not the case. Hybridisation is a cornerstone of customising evaluation designs and ensuring their appropriateness to different needs and circumstances. Most evaluators may see hybrid designs as mixing quantitative and qualitative methods in the same inquiry – perhaps adding case studies to management or monitoring evidence or participation and outcomes evidence. However, they can also mix methods within quantitative approaches, maybe by using different analytical techniques or sources to validate findings from programme management information or by using probability survey methods to supplement gaps in that information. Mixing different qualitative methods can also be highly valuable, using, perhaps, a series of focus group interviews to test issues and findings emerging from participant observation or a smaller number of in-depth case studies.

At the most practical level, mixing methods may be essential in filling some of the evidence gaps first identified when mapping information needs and assessing gaps in, for example, existing or secondary evidence sources. But beyond this, hybrid designs often offer evaluators more robust evidence, simply because any individual method of evidence collection will have limitations in how it reflects reality. Norman Denzin, one of the architects of current thinking and application of applied qualitative research methods, said of mixed mode approaches:

> No single method ever adequately solves the problem of rival causal factors. Because each method reveals different aspects of empirical reality, multiple methods of observations must be employed. (Denzin, 1970, p 28)

Combining different methods offers not just a practical and eclectic way of filling evidence gaps needs, crucially, it also offers a better chance of overcoming any limitations of relying wholly on single sources of evidence by drawing on evidence gathered using different approaches.

Observing or measuring each evidence need from multiple sources, through hybrid designs, draws on the concept of data *triangulation*. This provides stronger evaluation methodologies, often striking a balance between quantitative and qualitative information, and more confidence in conclusions. The idea of triangulation was borrowed over half a century ago (from geometry) drawing superficially on the approach by land surveyors (and map readers) to plotting an accurate single position by use of two (or more) separate landmarks. It was taken up earliest by quantitative researchers in the United States (Campbell and Fiske, 1959) but started to gain wider currency in social research (and later evaluation) through the early work of Denzin (Denzin, 1970). Others (Creswell, 1994, 2003) have outlined different approaches to the use of triangulation in research and evaluation, including:

- use of different data sources in the same enquiry;
- using different investigators in collecting and analysing (the same) evidence;
- harnessing different methods in analysing a single problem or programme;
- applying different theoretical perspectives to interpret evidence.

Any, and sometimes each, of these approaches can be relevant to particular evaluation needs.

Not everyone accepts the case for harnessing multiple methods and especially combining quantitative and qualitative modes. Some methodological purists may continue to urge caution in combining evidence-gathering methods that stem from different epistemological views. Some from within particular methodological paradigms have argued that this mixing of modes is incompatible with rigorous analysis (Mason, 2002). However, most in social research (Bryman, 2012), and in programme or policy evaluation, would now accept that this incompatibility is greatly exaggerated. Denzin and Lincoln (2000), two of social science's methodological giants, have gone so far as to propose multiple methods as one of their signature methodological rules for any and all research investigations.

Evaluators may not go quite so far, but in practical evaluation circumstances it would be rare to be able to make a case against mixing methods. It is probably only for evaluations taking place in highly controlled circumstances, where what is being evaluated is usually limited to a single and non-complex intervention, and typically for randomised control trials (RCTs; see Chapter 6), that hybrid designs are unlikely to be appropriate. Even for RCTs, as we shall see later, there are ways in which mixing methods through *nested evaluations* can add great value to measurement and understanding of the evidence.

Proportionality in design

If hybrid designs are one of the cornerstones of practical evaluation design, *proportionality* in making those choices is another. As we shall see from the next three chapters, those specifying or designing an evaluation are faced with a plethora of options and opportunities for making best use of evidence-gathering opportunities and needs. For secondary and primary evidence gathering, a key consideration is going to be whether and how use of sources and design choices are 'proportional' to the circumstances of what is being evaluated and the decision-making needs.

The idea of proportionality may seem straightforward, even common sense, since those commissioning an evaluation are unlikely to welcome an approach that is disproportionate. However, making proportionate choices in practice is a lot more challenging than it may seem. At its heart, it is about gearing choices about *robustness* of the methods to the nature and circumstances of the intervention that is being evaluated, not driving those choices by whatever budget or timetable is set.

Social researchers often speak of robustness of approach as an absolute, a level of evidence gathering and analytical rigor which is almost predetermined for particular circumstances. I doubt this is the case for any applied research, but for evaluation, robustness in choices of evidence-gathering approaches and analysis is geared largely to decision-making needs and the (very) different circumstances of what is to be evaluated. This is not pragmatism, a diversion to be avoided at all costs; it is about making choices that are appropriately proportionate to the evaluation circumstances and needs.

At the simplest level, no one would expect the scale and intensity of a summative evaluation of a small-scale, short-term pilot to match that of a longitudinal evaluation of a nationally rolled-out multi-strand programme. However, scale is only one factor in proportionality. While there is surprisingly little guidance on this cornerstone of successful evaluation, hard-won experience suggests proportionate choices are conditioned by eight features of whatever is being evaluated, as set out in Figure 3.2.

These are the most common influencing issues. Interventions come in a plethora of shapes and sizes, so the list is not exhaustive and evaluators will need to be on the lookout for other influences such as the sensitivity of evidence collection among vulnerable participants (or stakeholders).

Figure 3.2: Proportionality in different evaluation circumstances

Influence	Considerations in evaluation choices
High-profile interventions	High-profile, or innovative interventions or initiatives, and those expected to have a transformative or high impact, are likely to require thorough and quite probably large-scale evaluation evidence to build a sufficient evidence base on what works. This may also be needed for accountability for (large-scale) funding and to assess returns on investment (eg. to the public purse).
High level of intervention innovation or success risk	Highly innovative interventions (ie. high risk to policy makers and/or funders) are likely to require very high standards of evidence robustness (analysis and demonstrable validity) to show how well they are working in practice, as well as the quality of their impacts and the scale of returns/added value.
Short duration of intervention (or required evaluation)	Trial activities, fast turnaround pilot or intensive interventions, or summative evaluations which may not be commissioned until partway through an intervention, are all likely to be of limited duration. This will provide for more limited opportunities for data capture, comparison analysis over time or for longitudinal review, which will be reflected in the scale and depth of the viable evidence collection and review.
Large-scale or complex interventions	Larger-scale interventions are those with substantial investment which will (if for no other reason) probably require a more extensive and engaged evaluation to demonstrate that the money is well spent.
Small-scale or pilot/trial interventions	Pilot, trial or other small-scale interventions will have proportionality influenced more by the decision-making context (or immediacy) and/or by the likelihood (and evidence needs) to inform repetition, scale-up or rollout.
Need for wide generalisability of evidence from the interventions	Specific interventions may also be looked to for wider lessons or transferability and where an extensive evidence base may be needed to ensure that the results can be generalised with greater confidence.

Influence	Considerations in evaluation choices
Highly complex interventions	Multifaceted interventions (eg. multiple activities), or those addressing a variety of 'needs' or beneficiary circumstances, mean effectiveness or effects may be more difficult to isolate. Complexity means proportionate approaches are more likely to need to be extensive and sensitive to different user or application contexts.
Weak (no) existing evidence base for interventions	Where the existing evidence base is poor or under-researched, baselines are lacking, or comparative evidence is thin (or non-existent), an evaluation is likely to require more extensive application and evidence gathering to fill necessary gaps

Whatever influences affect any individual intervention, they are often overlapping. An intervention that is highly innovative, or at pilot scale may, for example, lack baseline or comparative evidence because of its novelty. Tackling these different circumstances, or combinations, will have implications for the type and level or resources likely to be required, and even for users' expectations of what the evaluation design can provide for decision-making. Making proportional choices will be a central feature of accommodating realistic needs and expectations.

A further design rule that has much to recommend it is that proportionality in choices should always lead resourcing (and funding) and not vice versa. Pragmatism may seem to suggest that proportionality helps to fit evaluation methods to the constraints of evaluation budgets or timeframes. This is a tempting but dangerous pathway. Resourcing is a real and present challenge to evaluators, especially when budgets and delivery timetables are set before an evaluator has the chance to start looking at appropriate designs. However, experience shows that where designers are caught in a needs–methods squeeze, proportionality in evaluation is an issue first and foremost for managing down (and perhaps renegotiating) expectations and objectives of an evaluation (as in Chapter 2) and not for streamlining evidence capture and analysis to fit budgets.

Data protection and security

Recognising the separate but related demands of data protection legislation and security for data-based evidence once it has been collected are increasingly sensitive aspects for evaluation design. Although interrelated, the two are usefully approached separately. The guidance offered here is generalised but will provide a sense of direction and a starting point for seeking more specific expertise or guidance.

Data protection

Compliance with regulatory requirements may be a very significant, or even a crippling constraint on evaluators' choices or execution of methods, so is best investigated early and thoroughly. This is especially true where fieldwork (survey or interview) for primary data collection is anticipated. Compliance needs can stem from organisational requirements, professional or other standards or codes of practice, but evaluators will usually be most affected by the effects of cross-national, federal or national regulation. This will affect their access to, and use of, personalised data, including names and addresses of individuals (for example, participants or beneficiaries of a programme being evaluated).

Regulations vary in scope, although they are harmonised in Europe under the EU Data Protection Directive of 1995, but they usually affect data on named individuals held on any computer system or relevant filing or record system. In the UK (via the Data Protection Act 1998) and most of Europe this does not apply to anonymised or aggregated data, although that is likely to be of little use for sampling purposes for evaluators wishing to collect additional, experiential or outcomes evidence from, for example, programme beneficiaries. Compliance centres on the individual or organisation (with a few exemptions) holding personal data; but this will affect evaluators when they are unable to secure access for data collection purposes to, for example, participants. Where affected in this way, evaluators may be able to negotiate with the data-holding organisation to either, for example:

- They may be able to deliver or distribute requests to participate on evaluators' behalf – and where through appropriate channels those responding (with appropriate briefing) can be assumed to have given informed consent to use of their personalised data.
- It may be possible to conduct the data gathering direct with participants – perhaps to a specified sampling requirement and using an agreed evaluation tool. For surveys, this would include any follow-up stages to boost responses and to ensure personalised data remain protected, including in (anonymised) survey returns.

Neither are ideal solutions and they will involve practical constraints on provider resourcing and capacities as well as some (and possibly considerable) bias in sampling, selection or evidence gathering. All of these will have implications (which will need to be accommodated) for the coverage and robustness of the analysis. Data protection requirements will also affect evaluators directly where they establish record systems that name individuals as part of evidence collection (for example, for follow-up stages in evidence gathering) and in handling the entitlement of data subjects (and in some cases third parties) to access 'their' data. Data protection can be a multifaceted and complex issue for evaluators. On the positive side, there is professional guidance (MRS and SRA, 2013) and guidance also to university-based evaluators (Charlesworth, 2014). For many evaluators this will usually be addressed in any ethics approval processes prior to commissioning (by contracting bodies) or pre-design, but it may also need specialist advice to ensure compliance.

Data security

At the other end of an evaluation, data security will be a significant issue for evaluators; but again, it is better considered early at the design and setup stages to avoid greater difficulties later on. This is all the more important when that data – participation records, feedback forms, data spreadsheets, client record management systems, individual (or aggregated) survey returns, electronic or hard copy questionnaires, interview records, case study or observation transcripts, or any identified narrative records – have personal identifiers recorded with (or identifiable from) them.

The forms of security needed will vary with the nature of the record or storage system and may well be specified by client or host organisations. Many public and commercial organisations will conform to specific international standards and client information security management systems or ISMS (ISO, 2015), and will have to ensure that any research or evaluation working with these will meet these standards. Data security may involve contingencies such as how long data will need to be kept and even how to deal with transcripts after the end of an evaluation, return of loaned record systems, destruction of utilised data or other requirements.

Those responsible for designing the evaluation may not feel comfortable with some of the technicalities. These are not covered here but there is no lack of expertise that can be harnessed to avoid what could be dangerous pitfalls later in the project.

Anticipating the analysis

A final issue for the compilation stage is looking at what is likely to be needed for the analysis. This may seem like 'jumping the gun'. It is not, and anticipating the requirements and expectations of the analysis of the different sources of evidence when it is collated can help ensure a smooth progression from evidence gathering to review and reporting. Experience suggests three main areas where a failure to anticipate what is needed for the analysis can pose problems later on:

- looking ahead to the necessary analytical capacity and skills sets needed;
- access to or suitability of any necessary comparative or contextual data;
- anticipating viable and appropriate analysis timelines and any needs for progressive analysis or staged review.

Analytical capacity and skills sets

Different forms of data and different forms of evidence collection are going to need different analytical skills sets. Complex evaluations and especially those using mixed methods may require a mix of analytical skills in the evaluation team. It is doubtful if an evaluation that will use complex regression methods to handle quantitative data sets, and will also undertake participant observation and multi-interview case studies, will find an individual with the skills necessary to handle those different analysis needs. Simpler evaluations may raise fewer challenges in terms of the analytical resources required, but will need to ensure that not only are the necessary skills available but also (to avoid delay to reporting) that they will be available when needed. Buying-in particular skills downstream – or even as an emergency resort at the last minute – risks not only analytical quality but also is likely to mean a loss of some of the contextual understanding that an established team member with the necessary skills would build up through the evaluation process.

Comparative or contextual data

Most forms of evaluation other than randomised control trials (where, as Chapter 6 shows, 'control' data is integrated into the mainstream evaluation process), will need some form of comparative, historic (for example, pre-intervention) baseline or contextual data to help the analysis make sense of the evaluation evidence gathered from within the intervention. Baseline information – the situation for whatever (or whomever) is being evaluated at the start of an intervention – is a common requirement, and an evaluation can do little to make sense of 'changes' or distance travelled across the intervention without it.

Baseline and other comparative evidence is usually provided from other sources – perhaps from the commissioning organisation, providers or official (for example, governmental, regulatory or other national) or non-official (for example, sectoral data) sources. It is tempting for evaluators to focus early on the primary data needs and design of evaluation tools, neglecting these comparative sources or pushing them downstream to be dealt with later. It is wise not to do so. Comparative data may need agreeing with client organisations, who will have views of what comparisons may be most relevant to their decision-making needs or circumstances (see Example 5).

Example 5: Evaluation of city-wide gambling addiction support services

A baseline evaluation was set up in one of the UK's largest metropolitan areas to review the scope and needs of problem gambling advisory and support services across different local agencies. The initiative followed an intensification of online and fixed odds betting terminal (FOBT) gambling and rising evidence of gambling-related harm, especially among some minority ethnic groups, as well as high-profile prosecutions of loan sharks preying on 'at risk' gamblers in those communities. A mixed-mode evaluation involved a variety of data being collected on gambling prevalence more generally and from advisory and support services locally, and also using appropriate comparative data to position trends and characteristics in the city.

A comparative methodology was developed for combining area data sets from the British Gambling Prevalence Survey (BGPS) and from gambling prevalence and harm indicators in the Health Survey for England (HSE) to provide comparisons, but this required close consideration of local authority social, economic and demographic data and matching to the BGPS and HSE data sets, to assess viable sample sizes and to agree which areas and combinations would be most appropriate. Anticipating the selection of these comparative areas required collation of indicator data and analysis of the official data sets, a standalone paper making recommendations, and discussion with the commissioning organisation and evaluation users, and was agreed two months into the five-month evaluation – timing that could only be accommodated as this was an early priority for the evaluation team.

Evaluators may also find gaps or inconsistencies between their primary data and its classification, and comparative data sets; these need to be anticipated if the coherence and credibility of the analytical contrasts are not to be compromised. They may also find it will take time to agree access to official data sets, or licenses may be needed to secure access. All this takes time – which evaluators may not have if they leave anticipating these needs to later in the evaluation process.

Timelines and staged review

It is common sense to acknowledge that good analysis takes time; rushing this stage may leave gaps or insufficiently considered findings and even lead to misleading conclusions. However, deciding on appropriate review and reflection time after data and evidence collation is not the only factor in anticipating analysis timing needs. Formative evaluations will need staged analysis but periodic review of early or interim findings may also be appropriate for longer duration 'summative' evaluations, looking at an intervention and its progression over time. Staged review can help build confidence and credibility among wider stakeholders and can be a valuable tool in building engagement in evaluations where the actions or outcomes of an intervention are high-profile or sensitive. Even where findings are not to be shared, progressive analysis can help the evaluators identify emerging issues and trends (perhaps from early quantitative evidence) to input to follow-up qualitative work through, for example, case studies – or vice versa.

In any of these areas, and others as well, a failure or delay in anticipating analysis needs early in the composition and design stage can compromise the credibility or quality of an evaluation's findings (and conclusions). Forewarned (about analysis needs) is indeed forearmed.

4

CONDUCTING PROCESS EVALUATION

- Understanding the different types of process evaluation and where to use them
- Distinguishing between process evaluation, self-evaluation and action research
- The focus of process evaluation – assessing achievements, effectiveness and quality
- Understanding the main options and choices for process evaluation methodologies
- Identifying and avoiding common pitfalls in conducting process evaluation.

Introduction

After the groundwork laid down by compilation and composition, evaluators come to conducting evaluation, with each of the three main types of evaluation considered in the following chapters. This chapter looks at process evaluations, which are often a gateway into professional evaluation where there are fewer immediate conceptual hurdles to the non-initiated than in economic or impact evaluations. The demand for process evaluations is widespread, and they remain the bedrock of understanding whether and how policies, initiatives and programmes are working, and how they might be improved.

Different types of process evaluation

As the name suggests, process evaluations concentrate on the working mechanisms of whatever is being evaluated. They are concerned with providing timely information on how well something is being, or has been, implemented against whatever expectations there are of it. Treasury guidance in the UK sees this as:

> a detailed description of what interventions are involved in a service or policy, who provides them, what form they take, how they are delivered and how they are experienced by the participants and those who deliver them. It can also provide an in-depth understanding of the decisions, choices and judgments involved, how and why they are made and what shapes this. (HM Treasury, 2011, p 82)

While this definition is geared towards central government civil servants looking at how well larger-scale government-funded actions and policies are working, it can equally apply to any attempt to stocktake how well smaller-scale or localised initiatives are being put in place.

Although there is not a uniform typology, some theorists have found it helpful to define different subtypes of process evaluations, variously in terms of 'implementation' evaluations, 'developmental' evaluations and 'managerial evaluations' (Ovretveit, 1998). Each of these usually takes place in an organisational context and *all* can be regarded as process evaluations. The differences are subtle and mainly in how the evidence to be generated is to be used.

Another difference is between process evaluations that are looking *downwards* from the decision-making needs of those funding or formulating an intervention, or *upwards,* often from the viewpoint of the organisation (perhaps a single provider) setting it up or delivering it. This difference between a top-down vs a bottom-up approach reflects scholarly thinking about important differences in organisational decision-making (Hill and Hupe, 2014). Downwards and upwards orientated process evaluations will be looking to gather different evidence, from different perspectives, and it is likely that these contrasts will need to be reflected in their methodologies.

Each of these different types of process evaluation share a common development-centred focus and in practice the contrasts between them are subtle. The different terms are often used inconsistently and consequently do not have much currency. In practice, they may be unimportant, as long as the approaches chosen reflect well-formulated objectives and anticipated use.

What is important in describing 'type' and the task involved is the difference between *summative* or *formative* process evaluations. A summative process evaluation is generally aiming to 'sum up' the results and effects of implementation, perhaps at the end of a funding or pilot period, or some other relevant endpoint. Summative evaluations do not have to be standalone, and often combine with an impact evaluation (although uncommonly with economic evaluations) to look at both processes and outputs and outcomes (see Chapter 6).

Formative process evaluations are more often standalone inquiries, and look at how something is working as it is being implemented, usually against preconceived expectations of early delivery. These can be conducted at any stage after start-up and usually at specific funding or improvement decision points for funders or providers. Some of the typical differences between summative and formative process evaluations are summarised in Figure 4.1 below.

Some might ask if a formative process evaluation that is also independent is not a contradiction. They might see a fundamental dichotomy between a formative evaluation aiming to inform change (in what is being evaluated) and the independence necessary for a credible and quality evaluation. However, while separation is crucial, the formative process evaluator can take steps to achieve and sustain this while still feeding back process evidence to help with improvement.

The distinction is subtle but important. A summative process evaluation can ensure independence by being fully detached from

Figure 4.1: Summative vs formative process evaluation

	Primary user(s)	Purpose	Reporting	Evaluator's role
Summative process evaluation	- Policy makers - Supervisory boards - Funders	- Resource/ funds accountability - End review of inputs/outputs from funding - Policy implementation review - Pilot rollout decisions - Performance management	- End of funding - End of pilot	- Independent - External - Detached
Formative process evaluation	- Fund managers - Sponsoring lead - Organisational managers	- Post start-up review - Mid-term health check - Staged audit - Short-term improvement	- Staged/ interim review - Mid-term progress review - Annual revie	- Inspectorial - External or internal - Independent or quasi-independent - Separated

the process, often reporting at or after the conclusion of what is being evaluated. A formative process evaluation cannot be detached in this way. Instead, it tackles independence differently by separating the evaluation and evaluators from the implementers (for example, programme providers) and decision makers. They adopt what amounts to an *inspectorial* role, working behind a 'glass wall' through which they observe, collect, analyse and interpret evidence, and inform improvement proposals, but which, at the same time, separates them from any subsequent decision-making about those improvements.

This separation is easier, and more credible, when there is a single stage of (formative) reporting and where formative evaluators are external to the intervention. With careful management, however, they can be conducted with multistage reporting and/or carried out internally where the evaluator is not a part of the delivery and decision-making team. The *Support for Excellence* case study in Example 6 below shows one way in which this was done.

Example 6: Glass walls and the evaluation of the National Support for Excellence Initiative

Public policy objectives aimed at the reform of technical education in England and Wales, saw government agencies setting up a programme for strategic Peer Review and Development (PRD) groups of top managers in each of over 300 further education institutions. This Support for Excellence programme, was rolled out through the Learning and Skills Improvement Service (LSIS) over three years to allow PRD groups to shape appropriate cross-institutional membership relevant to their own reform needs and national priorities. A national facilitation, networking and resource-sharing team, from an international management consultancy, supported these groups. Separately, an independent and formative process evaluation was set up and conducted externally, reporting each six months, first to inform start-up of the first 110 (Phase 1) PRD groups, then staged rollout and with a concluding review.

A three-way challenge for the evaluation was to be able to maintain independence while working closely with LSIS (to provide staged review of start-up expectations and speed of rollout), the facilitating team (regionally and nationally), and comparative evidence on implementation, enablers and constraints across PRD groups and at different stages of institutional and PRD group maturity. This was achieved by the evaluators agreeing a 'glass-wall' reporting protocol with LSIS. Data exchange and access requirements were built into the facilitating team contracts, and the evaluators drew evidence direct from PRD groups, cross-programme management information, provider surveys, and from 'fast start' case studies in the sector.

In addition to providing staged reports, the evaluators provided factual 'unpicking' briefings for both LSIS, the facilitating coordinating team and (through theme workshops) to early start PRD groups (subsequently through summary report distribution by LSIS) to explain evidence and better practice case study evidence. The glass-wall protocol meant that development implications (improvement proposals) set out in the reports were not discussed at these briefings beyond any issues of factual underpinning. The evaluators remained fully separated from improvement decision-making at all levels, or from commenting on decisions and priorities, but agreed improvement actions were notified to the evaluators and added to the review agenda for each subsequent evaluation report (to track progress).

As with the *Support for Excellence* example, process evaluation may be asked to combine formative and summative approaches. Experience suggests process evaluations are driven by one or the other; a summative evaluation may include staged reports for internal review but it remains an evaluation whose methods and timetable are geared to 'end-of-process' evidence and decision-making. On the other hand, a formative evaluation (as with *Support for Excellence*) may add a request for an end-of-evaluation report, drawing together previous staged (interim) reports, but this remains a formative evaluation at its heart to provide for improvement evidence as the evaluation progresses.

Although summative and formative process evaluations are rather different beasts, they share common ground and:

- are conducted independently, separated from delivery or implementation;
- are developmental in emphasis, providing specific evidence to support improvement of implementation (processes);
- have structured reporting to specific, anticipated, often fixed points geared to decision-making;
- audit actions and achievements against set expectations and/or a model process;
- inform improvement by going beyond measuring inputs and outputs to critically review how these were delivered and the change mechanisms.

These principles apply across circumstances, whether the evaluation is downwards or upwards looking, standalone or combined, one-off or staged reporting, formative or summative.

Process evaluation, self-evaluation and action research

Can a useful process evaluation be conducted in-house? I am often asked the question and the answer is a cautious (and conditional) 'yes'. The question hinges on the value of self-evaluation in its different guises over external, fully independent evaluation. This is not the place to look at the relative merits of self-directed over external evaluation (which alongside 'internal' evaluation, we have already covered in Chapter 2) but it is useful to look at the potential of self-evaluation where, unlike economic and impact evaluation, there is a much greater scope for use in process evaluation.

The reasons for this will be readily apparent to those facing these choices. In particular, self-evaluation can offer a much faster start, speedier turnaround, and may even be able to harness performance evidence in-house that may not be readily accessible if the evaluation is contracted externally. It will also be able to draw readily on detailed knowledge of the implementation, its circumstances, beneficiary groups and working relationships with stakeholders, which external evaluators may not. In addition, it will almost certainly be available at lower cost.

These are important drivers. Funders may even see a connection between process evaluation and action research within the intervention, and certainly both are concerned with using systematic evidence collected usually in real time for the purpose of informing actions. Action research, based on long-established ideas of reflective inquiry, has seen growing currency over the 70 years since the term was first coined (Lewin, 1946). As action-orientated and reflective research ideas and techniques have evolved, and become more rigorous, they have continued to share the idea of evidence collection and review by those engaged in the process of whatever is being changed or implemented.

Self-evaluation is not so very different, except in one crucial respect: action research may be centred on informing actions as something progresses, but its focus is on doing so by improved understanding and knowledge. Process (and other) evaluations have a similar aspiration, but their focus is not on improving knowledge but on providing specific evidence to inform decision-making and decision makers. Action researchers may be expected to be directly engaged in the decision-making; in contrast, evaluators, even self-evaluators, are not. While they may help unpick evidence and its implications, this stops (well) short of a direct role in decision-making. Indeed, self-evaluation will only be credible when the evaluators take, and can demonstrate, some of the steps talked about earlier to separate themselves from the effects of direct involvement in implementation.

So why aren't all process evaluations conducted through self-evaluation? The answers are usually in the credibility of what will emerge for those using the evaluation evidence. Self-evaluation will always have a harder time of establishing the validity of the interpretation of findings. Even where clearly separated from implementation, self-evaluators find it difficult to present themselves as independent. However much they demonstrate the currency of their knowledge of the intervention, the confidence of beneficiary groups, and in-depth understanding of how the policy or programme is being delivered, they will not be able to establish that they have avoided any conflicts of interest in the outputs of the evaluation. In short, for those users who might be suspicious of what is being proposed as efficiency changes or other improvements from the findings, they will always be open to the suspicion, however unfairly, of 'having an axe to grind'.

Where self-evaluation has greater currency and value, is where, for example:

- the evaluation is mandated as a self-evaluation, by policy makers or funders or in contractual obligations (for a subcontracted provider) or service-level agreement;

- the primary users of the evaluation findings are limited to decision-makers among executive or programme managers in a contracted provider or delivery organisation;
- the process evaluation has very limited aims, perhaps a stocktake of start-up or early achievements against contracted targets or goals.

So self-evaluation is possible, and in some circumstances even desirable, but it will involve risks – especially to credibility, confidence and utility of the findings – which need to be carefully weighed against the benefits.

Evaluating achievements

Process evaluations come in as many shapes and sizes as the interventions they aim to improve, but there is usually some common ground. This will include a need to evaluate:

- progress and achievements against goals and expectations;
- effectiveness of the intervention in achieving those goals, and often lessons learned;
- quality of the achievements and intervention against needs and expectations.

This is not to say these will be the only requirements, but they are the most commonplace. Each is looked at here, starting with evaluation of achievements.

Evaluating achievements is in many ways the most straightforward focus for a process evaluation. It would be very unusual if whatever was being evaluated did not have some pre-specified expectations, goals and even targets to act as the evaluation yardsticks. These typically might include:

- **Intervention goals or objectives:** These may perhaps be taken from a policy statement or implementation plan (for a directly delivered intervention) or from the original grant application, funding specification, terms of agreement or contract with a subcontracted provider(s) or programme management. A central or federal government initiated policy or programme might also have a written business case to help clarify goals. Where a logic chart or chain exists, it too will provide assumptions about goals (as well as inputs and outputs). All these will set out, for the evaluator, general expectations of achievements in what's to be done, who for, who with, and expected change or innovation.
- **Intervention inputs:** From the same or other documents can be drawn the hardwiring of the intervention, the inputs from grant or core (and discretionary) programme funds, matched or co-funding inputs (finance or direct staffing/secondments), delivery structures, staffing arrangements, start-up and delivery timetables (key milestones, overall timetable), collaborative arrangements and external engagements anticipated. These add up to the 'input' foundations of whatever is being delivered and where process evaluation looks at actual achievements to assess any shortfalls, causes and effects.
- **Intervention outputs:** These are the currency of what is expected to be achieved, usually deliverables or performance targets, perhaps in terms of recruitment, participation, retention, activities or actions put in place (from implementation, project or delivery plans, contracts or service-level agreements). These achievements may be at entry level (for example, applications, recruitment, programme admissions or starts), process achievements (for example, retention, renewals), or end-of-action achievements (for example, placements, qualifications, job entry, medical, heath or other social outputs).

Working with the available documentation will usually provide evaluators with an achievements map which can provide the framework for this part of a process evaluation; although what the documentation shows may need to be amplified by client/funder discussions. Account will also need to be taken of measurement and monitoring information to see what can be measured, as not all expected achievements may be readily quantified. From this it will be possible to identify key areas where additional evidence is needed from perhaps primary evidence collection (returned to below).

Looking at achievements may not be limited to goals, inputs and outputs of what is being evaluated. In large-scale programmes, process evaluation may be looking across different results from different areas, providers, client groups or economic sectors. Nearly all evaluations involve some comparative aspects. Process evaluations are no different, and policy makers, for example, will be interested in the bigger picture and will expect to see some evidence for whether and how results from a particular innovation contrasted with others. They may also be keen to see if achievement in the delivery model being evaluated outperforms others, or to better understand if what has been achieved by delivery in one context could be applied to another.

Evaluating effectiveness

Effectiveness of an intervention is often centre stage in a process evaluation but presents greater challenges than looking at achievements. A prerequisite is a clear and credible definition of what 'effectiveness' is expected to look like. This may have already been established for some process evaluations in arenas such as medicine, community or mental health, offender management or substance abuse, perhaps through a programme manual, protocol or other documentation. Elsewhere it may well be more vague, and there is real danger that evaluating effectiveness can end up with an open-ended expectation on evaluators.

Where 'effectiveness' is not demonstrably clear, the key is for evaluators to ignore the 'nice to know' and to focus down on precisely what needs to be looked at to inform intervention improvement. If evaluators are already familiar with the intervention area, stakeholders or likely beneficiaries' groupings, they may have enough knowledge already about what effectiveness might look like. If not, some work may be needed to pin down the primary users' expectations of what will be the key indicators of effectiveness, and what is measurable.

This will be a good starting point, but evaluating effectiveness as a process goes deeper than measuring single or a group of agreed indicators. Intervention effectiveness, especially in a policy or social context, is likely to be multifaceted, so to be useful, a process evaluation will need to look at it as the interaction between cause (the inputs and processes) and effect (the expected change and outputs). A useful start will be to unpick what effectiveness is expected to look like in terms of if/how the intervention has:

- been implemented as was anticipated by funders/policy makers; is there consistency with the intended delivery structure or model?
- used the anticipated resources appropriately and within any ring-fencing of key activities or other funding requirements (for example, participant eligibility);
- appropriately defined (and reached) its expected target population, including any specific actions aimed at direct or collaborative recruitment/engagement;
- delivered activities consistently with funders' expectations, plans or agreed priorities; have there been additional activities or processes contributing to implementation?
- achieved planned outputs within specification (for example, scale, timeframe) and to any service-level requirements; have there been additional or unexpected achievements?
- engaged effectively with stakeholders and/or partner organisations in the delivery arrangements;
- achieved the necessary developments or processes to deliver the innovation or changed practices expected of implementation;
- generated processes that have contributed in particular to achievements and implementation; what has worked particularly well?
- encountered processes that have held back or constrained achievements and implementation; what has worked less well?

If these are not already very clear from the evaluation specification, time can usefully be spent with the primary user, and perhaps other stakeholders, in clarifying which are important.

Not all of these will be relevant to specific interventions or the context of the evaluation. Others might be added to reflect particular expectations of effectiveness (for example, formative assessment of a new or pilot initiative). In each of these, effectiveness will not just be looking at achievements (against expectations) but also the gaps, reasons for gaps and the effects of any remedial or countermeasures in adjusting the delivery model. Above all, a process evaluation will be looking at the different faces of effectiveness not just through *measurement* of agreed indicators such as recruited participants, key activities delivered, and average waiting lists or response times, but also through *understanding* what has worked well and less well within those processes and why. This balance of quantitative and qualitative evidence is typical of process evaluations.

Effectiveness may also need to look at what outcomes and impacts have been secured, and this is looked at later (see Chapter 6).

Evaluating quality

The third common feature of process evaluations is the assessment of quality, and it is often the most difficult part. This relates not to evaluation of a quality control or assurance system in an intervention (although this may be required in some specialised evaluations); this is about the aspiration among the users or commissioners of an evaluation to take into account issues of the quality of an intervention, or participants' experiences of it.

Quality is also important because it adds a layer of understanding that might otherwise be neglected in favour of more readily assessed measures. A mid-term evaluation of a grant-aided programme to provide advice and guidance to homeless people, for example, might readily look at its achievements and effectiveness in service delivery, but looking at quality would go deeper. For example, this might set against hard indicators of performance quality, user views on:

- perceived accuracy, relevance or value of advice
- quality of access to service
- personalisation of initial assessment
- access to after-care support.

These may be seen as more 'soft' indicators of effectiveness, but put together with the harder edge measures, they provide for a more rounded picture. More generally, some of the particular needs and expectations of quality in process evaluations might include:

- consistency with quality compliance requirements affecting an intervention as set by regulatory or other bodies;
- the gap, and its causes, between higher and lower quality delivery within and between different providers or different participant groups;
- integrating an end user perspective alongside those of managers and professionals;
- going beyond targeted performance measures or compliance requirements;
- consumer- or user-facing information that might be used later (by funders or providers) to help future users make more informed choices about access and use.

If lucky, process evaluators may find some very specific requirements that set out what 'quality' is meant to look like, perhaps in a service-level agreement to providers, in a contract or quality plan, or by reference to external service or regulatory standards. However, they may be facing more intangible definitions or a situation where different stakeholders have different views (or priorities) over what different aspects of quality mean to them. Intangible (or different) expectations of quality need first to be clarified and reconciled, and shown to be measurable and credible. If those commissioning the evaluation have not provided for this, a starting point might be to look at minimum quality expectations or requirements, for example:

- participants' accessibility to the service or activities supported through the intervention (including online accessibility for e-services);
- relevance or appropriateness to service-level and/or participants' needs;
- equity of treatment/engagement across different groups' needs;
- service-level acceptability (what is provided, how and where/when);
- effectiveness in terms of delivering required outputs (outcomes);
- efficiency in terms of resource use, waste minimisation and cost-effectiveness;
- efficacy in terms of producing the required change or utility of output;
- responsiveness of provision/actions to service-level needs and/or expectations;
- sustainability or continuity of service or intervention.

This is a long list; particular quality issues in specific intervention circumstances might well make it longer.

Methodological options and choice

Getting to grips with achievements, effectiveness and quality, as well as other aspects of a process evaluation, presents the evaluator not only with diverse evidence needs but also many options for how to meet these. These choices are further complicated because process evaluations commonly need to look across, and take evidence from, different sources to contrast the experiences of different players and, typically:

- evidence from those funding it, or setting expectations and/or closely associated stakeholders;
- evidence from those at the front end of delivering the intervention, including providers;

- evidence from those directly engaged in the programmes – the participants and recipients;
- evidence, often also from the end users – those who may not be directly participating but will be the beneficiaries of whatever the intervention is aiming to change.

Different evidence will be needed across these groups and where the precise information needs will have been mapped by establishing the key indicators to measure across achievements, effectiveness and quality. Heterogeneous sources of evidence, and varying (key) information needs will require distinct (or differently applied) methods. For most process evaluations, making the 'right' methodological choices is consequently likely to involve a mix of methods, including both quantitative and qualitative techniques (with which it is assumed readers will already be familiar) with a range of such methods and where:

Quantitative methods will be most likely to be used to provide the necessary hard edge to a process review and in particular in measuring key process variables across achievements, effectiveness and quality. They are also likely to be a foundation for testing an intervention's success, perhaps comparatively against past practice, or similar initiatives with wider (for example, national) benchmarks. A starting point will be the available secondary evidence, usually from monitoring, management or performance information (from the intervention). This will often be collected routinely by providers or as a contractual requirement, but is unlikely to meet all evaluation needs. There may be some shortfall in the scope, coverage or accuracy of the evidence, or in how up to date the available information is, and mapping these gaps (see Chapter 3) will inform what is desirable for primary quantitative data collection (for example, through surveys or other additional data collection methods).

Qualitative methods will be important in taking a process evaluation beyond measurement to provide for a complementary understanding of the decisions, choices, judgements and different experiences of participants and partners, and how these were implemented. Quantitative data will contribute to this, but can only go so far. The qualitative input may come from methods as diverse as structured and semi-structured interviews, focus groups, narrative analysis, observations and various forms of case studies, often used in different combination across the different players. Again, these methods are not discussed here in any detail; it is assumed readers will have familiarity with their appropriate use or will take the steps necessary to achieve this.

One methodological issue that does deserve more detailed consideration is the use of *participatory* evaluation methods in providing for some of the information needs. An odd combination of cost pressures and new research paradigms such as participatory action research (PAR) provides opportunities for process evaluators to put stakeholders, including beneficiaries, centre-stage in evidence collection and perhaps evidence review. This means the evaluators will find themselves combining the roles of evidence collectors and analysts with facilitating intervention participants to be an active part in the process review.

Although sharing much with PAR principles (Attwood, 1997; Kemmis and McTaggart, 2005), and offering great scope for more creative evidence collection methods (Kara, 2016), the ambition of participatory evaluation is generally much more restricted. PAR's principle goes beyond engagement of communities of interest, with particular knowledge and strengths to offer what has been called:

> a radical alternative to knowledge development ... a collective, self-reflective inquiry for the purpose of improving a situation. (MacDonald, 2012, p 37)

Participatory methods are not limited to process evaluation, and they may not be appropriate to some sensitive evaluations, or welcomed by all commissioners. However, they can be an important aid to the process evaluator, on their own (as in Example 7 below) or alongside other methods. Participatory approaches can also open up different experiences and interpretations, and lines of enquiry and interpretation that might have remained hidden by relying wholly on mainstream primary and secondary sources. They can also increase the credibility of the evaluation, especially within a policy environment where active engagement of beneficiary communities may boost confidence in, and the influence of, evaluation findings (see Chapter 7).

Example 7: Using participatory methods to evaluate the provision of calorie information by catering outlets

As with many national and federal governments, successive administrations in the UK have been concerned to tackle diet-related public health issues, including the rise in obesity and type 2 diabetes. An early initiative was to provide nutrition information in retail catering outlets, specifically calorie labelling, and to test the viability of this the Food Standards Agency (FSA) launched a small-scale initiative with 21 retail businesses to make calorie information (CI) available to consumers at the point of choice (POC). An FSA process evaluation was set up to explore the effectiveness of these first steps and to develop an early understanding of consumers' use and understanding of the scheme, and to show where improvements could be made. The novelty of the initiative, and its relatively small scale, saw evaluators and users agreeing on a focus on participatory evaluation methods to embrace different stakeholder views. This included:

- semi-structured telephone or face-to-face interviews with senior and programme managers in 20 of the 21 head offices of the volunteer retail businesses; these included looking at setup, CI display decisions, improvements and the scope for wider rollout of a voluntary scheme;
- parallel interviews with POC (outlet) general managers in 19 of these businesses to assess frontline sales experience on effectiveness and effects, and the scope for improvement;
- customer research (289 interviews) across POCs – 143 POC observational interviews where consumers were asked about how they were choosing their food, and 146 post-choice interviews after people had made food choices – to better understand CI display from user perspectives and use of CI in making decisions;
- eight group discussions with consumers in four locations to unpick specific issues raised in the customer interviews.

The findings were used to develop proposals for national rollout of a voluntary CI labelling scheme and a subsequent consultation prior to rollout.

(Case study after HM Treasury, 2011)

For all these benefits, use of participatory evidence collection is not cost or risk free. Direct beneficiary inquiry is likely to involve mainly qualitative sources such as participant diaries, storytelling, case studies, and, of course, semi-structured or unstructured interviewing which may be evaluator or participant led. These tend to be resource and analysis intensive. They will also likely raise challenges of appropriate selection of the evaluation participants to reflect whatever focus is needed – for example, better practice, representation or thematic illustration to highlight particular process issues or effects such as that of generic eligibility rules on the participation of particular minority groups.

Avoiding pitfalls in process evaluation

Process evaluation may well be the starting point for those coming into evaluation for the first time. It does not present the conceptual challenges of economic or impact evaluation but it has its fair share of practical pitfalls to avoid. It will help to clarify thinking if evaluators start by asking the following questions:

- Is there clarity about what is being evaluated in the intervention, the intervention period and actions (processes)?
- Is there sufficient understanding of the intervention context, policy expectations and why its 'processes' are being evaluated now?
- What are the improvement expectations underpinning the evaluation? Are they realistic in terms of what the evaluation can look at and assess?

- Are these expectations consistent with what is being asked for, either as a formative assessment or a summative process evaluation?
- If it is a self-evaluation, are the glass walls recognised, credible and likely to be effective; has clear separation been provided for the evaluators?
- Are there clear, credible and agreed definitions of what is being focused upon as regards achievements, effectiveness and quality, and any other key considerations, and has there been engagement with the primary user (and stakeholders) in building that clarity?
- Is there confidence that the responses to all of these questions are reflected in a methodological focus that is appropriate and proportionate to meeting needs?

If these questions have been tackled fully and honestly, along with others that might be more specific to the evaluation, evaluators should be confident that they are well placed to ensure they will be conducting and delivering a well-focused and useful process evaluation. The evaluation should also be potentially well placed to deal with any unexpected snags or additional expectations that might arise – as is often the case – as it is put in place and progresses.

5

CONDUCTING ECONOMIC EVALUATION

- Placing economics into evaluation practice via the four types of economic evaluation
- Simple economic evaluations looking at cost description and cost minimisation
- Cost-effectiveness and cost avoidance approaches in evaluation
- Cost-utility evaluations
- Cost-benefit evaluations
- Using sensitivity analysis to strengthen economic evaluation
- Avoiding common pitfalls in economic evaluation

Introduction

A well-designed process (or impact) evaluation can show accountabilities and how well a policy has worked against expectations, but it will not demonstrate objectively whether the outputs and outcomes justified the funding or investment that went into it in the first place. Economic evaluations look precisely at those issues, including whether or to what extent those costs were outweighed by the benefits. Not all economic evaluations will be specialist, standalone affairs, and they can be combined with a process or impact evaluation to pay some attention to the resources expected to be used in an intervention, as well as their costs and how these relate to the benefits arising. More sophisticated needs such as cost-benefit associations are not without their critics, and harnessing the most appropriate approaches will need specialist, standalone designs if their findings are to be credible and useful.

Understanding the economic perspective

Economic evaluation is about much more than reducing the inputs, outputs and outcomes of an intervention to numbers and into money values (monetisation). A well-balanced economic evaluation goes beyond numbers to critically review the often unconscious assumptions and choices made in setting up interventions and delivering them. It also draws attention to the fact that the funding and resources committed to an intervention could be allocated to other things, and the true costs (direct and indirect) and value, often need to be understood if judgements are to be made about future investment. In the modern world, this may loom large where decision makers are juggling multiple priorities and scarce resources.

A starting point to conducting economic evaluation that can cast light on these wider issues is an understanding of some of the deeper principles that underlie economic evaluation. Economic evaluation may be a highly quantified process but one where reducing inputs/outputs and outcomes to numbers is itself almost always value-laden, and needs to allow for seen and unseen effects.

It is also usually not enough to just balance the costs of inputs and particular outputs of an intervention. This may be fine for an economic evaluation looking no further than intervention accounting, where the only question is, 'have the time and budget put in place been used by the activities and users as expected?' However, most economic analysis expects more. Even the concept of 'value' is relative, so an economic evaluation is also likely to need to show (comparatively) how the same or a similar level of resource might have been used more (or less) effectively in a different way and usually through assessing the *opportunity costs*. It is this broader way of looking at costs, values and consequences that complicates the situation – and the designs needed for most approaches to economic evaluation.

Opportunity cost is a fundamental principle of (micro) economic theory. In the real world, resources are not infinite, so to fully appreciate how they are used it is necessary to relate scarcity of resources to the choices made in using them. Economists have developed sophisticated methods of doing this through quantifying the cost of *not* enjoying the benefit that would have occurred if an alternative choice had been made. This is referred to in economic theory as the *best alternative output forgone*. This can be looked at, by way of illustration, through the eyes of a participant on, for example, a piloted new work-skill qualification: they may gain a measurable benefit (a higher level qualification) from taking part, but in doing so they may forego other things, for example, through loss of income or earnings as a result of taking time out of work to attend.

This loss of a potential (alternative) gain is the opportunity cost to the participants, and to understand the true economic cost of an intervention it needs to be set against whatever benefit they did secure from participation. Economic evaluation will need to scale up this potential loss to cover all participants and also different forms of opportunity costs (not just loss of earnings to someone in work), going beyond simple financial costs of money earned (or not earned). The real cost of an alternative output foregone may be in less tangible things such as lost time. However, even those intangibles need to be translated into money values (where possible) if the evaluation is to be comparable and make sense to decision makers.

Considered in this way, economic evaluation is just a way of looking comparatively at an intervention to allow for the costs and consequences of alternative choices or courses of action. There are different ways of doing this according to the circumstances of an intervention and the needs or ambition of users about what evidence is needed, with four broadly different approaches to economic evaluation:

- cost-description evaluation (including something called cost minimisation);
- cost-effectiveness evaluation
- cost-utility evaluation;
- cost-benefit evaluation.

These are much more than increasingly higher levels of approaches (although cost–benefit approaches are a great deal more complex than cost description). They are different evaluation approaches to different evaluation needs. Figure 5.1 shows one way of looking at these differences by contrasting the approaches' scope and coverage of inputs/outputs/outcomes/impacts.

Figure 5.1: Applying the main types of economic evaluation

Intervention features	Cost-description evaluation	Cost-effectiveness evaluation	Cost-utility evaluation	Cost-benefit evaluation
Inputs	√	√	√	√
Processes	√	√	√	√
Outputs		√	√	√
Outcomes		√	√	√
Impacts				√

So economic evaluation approaches move from the simpler focus of cost description evaluation (only costing resources used in inputs and processes of whatever is being evaluated), to a full-scale, and usually very complex, cost–benefit evaluation. The more complex approach looks at the full spectrum of resources used and benefits and changes secured, set against the opportunity costs and benefits of alternative possible actions. A cost-benefit evaluation also moves away from looking at costs to the more complicated area of valuation, a contrast in economic thinking that we shall look at shortly. The rest of this chapter looks at where these very different pathways to economic evaluation relate to different needs and circumstances.

A final consideration before looking at the different approaches is when an economic evaluation is conducted, and this comes down to two essential choices (Rossi et al, 2004):

- an ex ante (or prospective) economic evaluation, which is conducted before an intervention has been implemented;
- an ex post (retrospective) evaluation, which takes place after an intervention has started and can be either formative (part or midway through) or summative (at or close to the end, or at a concluding point for decision makers).

Both require assumptions to be made, with ex ante evaluations looking at what the likely costs and benefits will be before an investment is made, and an ex post looking at actual costs and benefits, but needing to make many assumptions about how to quantify these. Ex ante economic evaluations tend to be associated with larger scale and often prospectively publicly funded investments. However, they can also be helpful in a systematic approach to evaluation because of the insights they can provide (including on the validity of cost and benefit and quantification assumptions) for a subsequent ex post evaluation.

Much more could be said about the underpinning concepts – 'financial' vs 'economic' costs, marginal costs, market and non-market costs and value, revealed and stated preferences – but this is not the place to digest economic theory. This chapter aims to provide a starter for prospective evaluators, in order to demystify what may seem a complex and unapproachable aspect of evaluation, not to turn readers into readymade experts of cost-benefit assessment methodologies (which might take a little more time and many more words).

Cost evaluations

As Figure 5.1 shows, cost evaluation is the simplest form of economic evaluation. It is most likely not to be a standalone evaluation, but conducted as a part of an ex post process evaluation, either as formative or summative evaluation. Its focus is on the resources used in delivering an evaluation, describing actual and net costs (taking account of, for example, expenditure on an intervention against any fees or revenue drawn in), but goes little further, and usually takes little or no account of the outputs and no account at all of benefits or outcomes.

Although the most straightforward approach, cost evaluations come with different levels of complexity. A standalone cost evaluation will look just at the intervention, through an essentially descriptive exercise, although this might set actual costs against those proposed, to set out any cost savings achieved or overrun. Analysing costs is not quite as straightforward as may first seem to be the case, and evaluators are likely to need to distinguish between those summarised in Figure 5.2 below.

Figure 5.2: Scope of costs to be included in a cost evaluation

Nature of costs	Scope	Example
Fixed costs	Costs that are constant over a specific period of time (eg. annual or financial year) irrespective of volume of activity	Rental costs for premises, salary and on-costs for 'permanent' staff (not sessional), annual contract hire fee for equipment
Variable costs	Costs tht vary within a specific time period or according to the volume of activity	Maintenance costs not covered by 'fixed' maintenance contract support
Semi-variable costs	Costs that include a fixed and variable element	Costs of sessional staff where this includes an annual retainer fee (fixed) and hourly or sessional costs according to time engaged (variable)
Step costs	Costs that do not change steadily with changes in activity or volume, but rather at discrete points – a fixed cost within certain boundaries, outside of which it will change	Costs of premises that are fixed up to a requirement for a maximum number of staff or visitors (eg. intervention participants) but which will change when capacity is exceeded and additional premises are needed

Variable, semi-variable and step costs are sometimes referred to as incremental costs (although some economists would argue that over time all costs are incremental). All are part of a cost evaluation and the challenge for conducting this is to be able to be as comprehensive as possible and to account for all appropriate costs over the evaluation period.

What is being evaluated will be driven by multiple inputs and different sorts of resources, so when evaluating costs there is quite likely to be a need to make judgements about what it is sensible to include and what it is not. A trade-off may be required between what effort is needed to collect some information and its significance to the overall costs of an intervention. Similarly, sensible judgements may also have to be made on what indirect costs it is appropriate to include, with service marketing and staff training likely to be important, but depreciation costs of systems or equipment possibly not (unless what is being evaluated involves substantial capital investment as a start-up cost).

Other considerations are additionality and apportionment of costs. Many interventions may be run by subcontracted providers, in which case some allowance needs to be made for what costs are genuinely additional to the provider – which would not have otherwise occurred if the delivery relating to the intervention had not taken place. Conversely, some apportionment of costs may be needed, perhaps for the time of senior managers or other professionals (for example, IT, procurement or HR managers) who will not be directly involved in delivering the intervention and may be putting in only a small amount of their time on an occasional basis, but who nonetheless make up an element of the resources used. Just as with accounting and auditing, a variety of *intangibles* may also need to be agreed and included.

The time period of a cost evaluation needs to be appropriate, since costs measured over a (too) short time period risk being distorted by unusual events (for example, high levels of staff turnover and recruitment costs early in the new year, staff cover costs during the summer vacation period). Short time periods may also risk higher costs, for example, as the use of staff or equipment takes time to bed down after a start-up phase.

There is no template for what is included and what is not included in a cost evaluation, and what the viable time periods are for fair cost assessment. Different interventions will, of course, have a variety of resources available (and different ways of using them). What is included will depend on the particular needs and perspective of an evaluation, issues that are best agreed early to avoid any misunderstandings or misplaced expectations (see Chapter 2).

Sometimes a cost evaluation might also involve a comparative look at the costs of similar activities to set out relative costs of an intervention. Comparative cost descriptions are sometimes referred to as *cost-minimisation* evaluations. As well as looking at overall costs, they may attempt to contrast the costs of different forms of action within a single (or multiple) intervention. For example, a process evaluation looking at a newly introduced advice and helpline for vulnerable people might compare overall and unit costs for the telephone helpline, in contrast to the resourcing of a parallel web chat room in the same service, and elective e-guidance sessions for users. The evaluation may perhaps set all these against costs for supplying problem-resolution information and materials on the service website.

Cost-effectiveness evaluations

A common mistake among those specifying an evaluation is to ask for a cost-benefit evaluation when what they actually need is a (narrower) cost-effectiveness focus; these are quite different things. Cost-effectiveness evaluations go one step further than cost evaluations by looking also at costing what comes out of an intervention. Cost-benefit evaluations (looked at separately below) go even further than nominal costs to review the value of outcomes. Both cost-effectiveness and cost-benefit evaluations can be conducted as ex ante or ex post evaluation, but are most common as a retrospective (ex post) economic evaluation. Both routes increase the scope and usefulness of the evaluation to decision makers, but this comes at a price, with many more assumptions needing to be factored in.

The essence of cost-effectiveness analysis is being able to relate the costs of implementing and delivering the intervention to the value of the outputs and outcomes generated. Occasionally a cost-effectiveness evaluation may be limited to inputs and outputs (for example, for an interim evaluation or a formative approach) but this is only a halfway house to understanding cost-effectiveness if it does not also look at outcomes. Results from a cost-effectiveness evaluation are typically set out as an estimate of the cost per unit of output/outcome. These 'unit costs' are the most straightforward way of simplifying cost-effectiveness, and they can be applied, and readily compared, across all sorts of different activities. Picking which unit costs to focus on depends on the purpose of the intervention, so, for example, a programme centred on improving opportunity for disaffected young people by returning to education might have unit costs based on the cost per new qualification achieved, and a homeless initiative might have costs per homeless person obtaining a secure tenancy.

Cost-effectiveness evaluation may focus on particular aspects of monetised efficiency including, for example, costs not incurred or saved as a result of an intervention – cost avoidance. Example 8 below shows how these methods, and a unit-cost approach, were used to estimate the cost-effectiveness of a public service vehicle driver safety programme.

Example 8: Drivermetrics and Arriva Group cost-avoidance evaluation of improving driver safety assessment and training

Following concerns about the need to enhance Public Service Vehicle (PSV) safety training, Drivermetrics, at Cranfield University, and Arriva, a major public transport company operating in the UK and across Europe, developed the Bus Driver Risk Index (BDRI) as an assessment tool. BDRI was piloted in Arriva's North West Group, and pending a national rollout, the cost-effectiveness of the combined BDRI online tool, supplementary safety training and coaching was evaluated in 2014 through a cost-effectiveness evaluation.

The evaluation aimed to quantify cost avoidance for the company and drew on comparative driver accident data three years before and after BDRI use. This showed a reduction (2010–12) of 9% for all accidents and a greater reduction of 25% fewer in 'at fault' accidents. Using parallel data for other Arriva regions (not involved in the pilot), the evaluation estimated a net reduction of 2.2 of 'at fault' accidents per driver in the three-year test period. It also estimated substantially reduced costs from vehicle damage and off-road losses to capacity and reduced passenger injury/compensation levels.

Cost-effectiveness was projected from these 'net' impacts by assessing cost avoidance based on unit costs for PSV accidents (based on a standard claims reserving measure). This estimated net cost avoidance of £308,000 over 2010–12 for the NE region alone after adjusting for the incurred costs of BDRI assessment and coaching. Further cost avoidance was also identified for improved staff retention, reduced driver absence and reduced costs from vehicle damage and off-road losses to capacity, but these were not included in the cost avoidance estimate because of the lack of region-level data that could be monetised. The evaluation also showed strong additionality and no evidence of deadweight in the estimated cost avoidance.

As the Arriva example shows, using unit costs as an indicator of cost-effectiveness is almost always about estimation – not measurement. The assumptions that have to be made to relate intervention costs to outputs or outcomes mean that whatever unit costs come out of the evaluation, these are best estimates and not precise measurements.

The value of using unit costs is that while much of the economic jargon may not be well understood by evaluation users, unit costs are readily grasped – it costs X amount of money to get one of Y. However, they can have a spurious credibility and the reliability of the estimate(s) depends on the combination of the appropriateness of the different assumptions made and the quality of the data harnessed. The assumptions and data limitations also need to be shared with users, alongside the unit-cost(s) estimated, so they can judge for themselves the quality of the estimation.

A cost-effectiveness evaluation will typically focus on a single or targeted output or outcome relevant to that particular intervention (reduced PSV accident incidents in Example 8). No attempt is made to look at the wider value or that from multiple outputs or outcomes, and where this is important a cost-benefit evaluation is more appropriate. For example, a pilot programme in a single city or region of 'credit' finance support to first-time small-firm exporters, might be interested in the cost-effectiveness of providing credit guarantees (the selected output) because this will guide what aspects of the service can be rolled out nationally within a fixed budget. Here the cost-effectiveness evaluation may be looking at the unit costs of achieving the specific output (a business credit guarantee) through different actions in the same pilot programme – perhaps agreed credit contracts from a telephone assistance helpline, an online application and documentation system, and F2F 'on-site' advisory sessions. In this way, cost-effectiveness can be evaluated for different alternative forms of support and to compare which has the greater relative effect (efficiency) on achieving the output measure within the intervention.

The strength of cost-effectiveness evaluation is this focus on comparative analysis for a chosen output, and being able to condense effectiveness to show that spending x money will result in y benefit. However, this simplicity (of concept if not application) is also its weakness. Relying on a single measure for setting that X to Y measure of £, € or $ cost-effectiveness will open the evaluation, and the evaluator, to risks in terms of the usefulness of that single measure or the validity of the data harnessed for the comparisons. The real challenge is in picking the most useful output measure for this sort of comparison, an issue that may need negotiation with the decision makers and perhaps wider stakeholders.

Cost-utility evaluations

Cost–utility evaluation is a variation on cost-effectiveness methods. It is worth looking at separately, because it has particular use for public and community health, wellbeing and medical evaluations. Here, utility is used in a very specific way to value (as opposed to costing) outputs or outcomes, and it is particularly useful where interventions concern non-market goods or services.

Economists look at 'utility' in terms of quantifiable value to an individual and in particular in terms of the *total satisfaction experienced by a consumer* of goods or services or in terms of a change in their wellbeing. Used in this way, utility is an important part of rationale choice theory, an idea almost as old as classical economic theory itself, and where the concept underpins individuals' ability to make logical and prudent choices. To the evaluator, utility focuses on the effect of the evaluated activity measured in terms of how beneficiaries, end users or others participating (the 'consumers') value that effect. It is a participant-facing measure and one of particular value for some evaluations with a highly personalised or perhaps community focus.

Utility has been used by researchers to explain what motivates individual behaviours in areas as diverse as criminology, discrimination, gambling, labour market and human capital studies, but its use by evaluators has remained largely confined to health and, especially, medical studies. Here it has been used to better understand the relative value of innovations and especially new medical treatments, and to move away from traditional output measures such as lives saved or extended years of life to a patient-centred view based on quality of life. In most uses, cost-utility, unlike cost-effectiveness, cost avoidance (or cost benefit), means the evaluator will have little (or no) discretion in choosing the utility measure. This is most likely to be derived from specialised 'consumer' valuation indicators, with one of the most common medical or health utility measures being the 'quality adjusted life year' (QALY) measure; another is the 'healthy day equivalent' – both expressed as money values.

Specialists in health evaluation have long observed that cost-utility could have much wider application (Ovretveit, 1998). There have been some developments in this area (Dolan and Peasgood, 2007) in areas such as costs of criminality on victims, but these methods remain, as yet, little used in the policy environment (outside health). However, by providing a user-based valuation, cost–utility could have considerable potential in taking account of wider economic considerations now gaining currency, such as individuals' wellbeing.

Cost-benefit evaluations

Cost-benefit evaluations are not for the faint-hearted and specialist economic expertise is needed for these to be effectively designed and conducted. Nevertheless, understanding the basic principles is important to anyone making choices about which types of economic evaluation may be needed. The focus here is not on precise application, which would be ambitious for the likely readers of this book, but on the role and potential of cost-benefit assessment methods for the purposes of understanding the value of programmes, policies and interventions. Nor do we look at where cost-benefit assessment can be put to equally good use in, for example, assessing prospective investment decisions in the public sector (HM Treasury, 2013) or elsewhere.

Cost-benefit evaluations start with deciding on specific viewpoints from which the economic assessment and analysis is shaped. The viewpoint taken may already be decided when evaluators come to a specification that is already written, but for those preparing the goals, objectives and focus, this viewpoint taken will influence the precise indicators and assumptions subsequently made (Drummond et al, 2005). Viewpoints usually come from those providing or funding the resources, and commonly may be individual (self-funding) participants, grant awarders or other intervention funders, or perhaps a central or federal government agency, or state or local government funding an intervention.

This type of evaluation can be conducted ex ante or ex post and, in both cases, can move away from a focus on prospective or actual 'costs' to an attempt to value the consequences of a programme in monetary terms. Like cost-effectiveness evaluations, they are concerned with inputs, outputs and outcomes but also, possibly, with valuing longer-term consequences and impacts from the intervention. Unlike cost-effectiveness evaluations, they centre on placing a monetary value on the changes in outcomes (for example, the value of placing a homeless person into a secure tenancy and accommodation). This is more than a shift in technique and means that cost-benefit approaches can start to critically review the overall justification for an intervention – do the benefits incurred outweigh the costs involved?

This will involve quantifying as many of the costs and benefits of a policy as possible and setting values to these. So for a homeless-placing intervention to set benefits against the costs (direct and indirect), a cost benefit evaluation will need to value a range of conceivable gains to the health and wellbeing of individuals no longer sleeping on the streets or in temporary shelters, and associated benefits such as enhanced access to employment (from acquiring a stable address). It is also likely also to look at *externalities*: the outcomes for individuals who are not directly involved in the intervention, but who are affected (indirectly). Compared to a cost-effectiveness analysis, cost-benefit evaluation can provide a much more rounded assessment of what is being evaluated and its wider social costs and benefits.

In all of this, the end purpose is to explain if the benefit of an evaluated intervention is greater or smaller than its cost. While this aim may be simple enough, meeting it in practice can require very complex quantitative analysis, unpicking the processes and assumptions within delivery to identify and isolate a full range of measurable costs and benefits, and making further assumptions about how to translate those monetary values. A good starting point will be to see if other research or evaluation might provide ready measures that can be used or adapted: perhaps analogous work on *value for money* measures in similar activities, or interventions to that being evaluated.

If ready or proxy values are not available to cost-benefit evaluations, the evaluators will need to make choices and rationalise any assumptions they are making, to provide for a full spectrum assessment of all costs (including opportunity costs), direct and indirect, and benefits. Typically a wider range of benefits will be valued, and here there is (again) no template for what to include, or how and what assumptions to make. All this needs to be built up as the framework for the cost-benefit measurements, so that it is geared precisely to the circumstances of what is being evaluated.

Obviously this is a technically demanding form of evaluation. It is further complicated by the fact that this is not a value-free process, with evaluators needing to make numerous and reasoned assumptions not just about what is to be included but about how to value these. Conduct of a cost-benefit evaluation will also be about testing these assumptions, and critically reviewing the effects on the analysis of suitability (and alternative choices or values). Cost-benefit evaluators will also need to explain fully these processes and assumptions in the final reporting, with all this adding to the complexity of the analysis.

In short, if they are to be done robustly, cost-benefit evaluations require a very extensive framework of cost and benefit assumptions before any analysis is attempted, as well as transparency in how those assumptions are made. Many, or perhaps most economic evaluations, or evaluations where there is economic assessment content, do not need this focus or level of complexity. Where they do, it is a tall order, and (as we shall see for randomised controlled trials in Chapter 6) should only be undertaken where there is confidence that the necessary broad spectrum of costs and benefits can be taken into account by means of reliable data or estimation.

Any assessment looking across cost-benefit evaluation needs also to recognise the potential of harnessing some of the specialist approaches developed, and in particular social return on investment (SROI). SROI has roots in social enterprise, building on the logic of cost-benefit analysis but aimed at valuing social and environmental impacts which may not be fully covered in more conventional approaches. This has become a distinct and partly commercialised approach, guided by members of the Social Value UK network (formerly the SROI network). SROI involves very specific techniques and training, with the seven underlying principles and specific methods set out first in a UK Cabinet Office Guide in 2009, since updated (Nicholls et al, 2012). These methods have developed currency in and around the third sector, where they remain a valued approach for very specific economic evaluation needs.

Sensitivity analysis

No discussion of economic evaluation is complete without looking at the value and role of sensitivity analysis (sometimes referred to as sensitivity testing). Sensitivity analysis is not confined to economic evaluation, or to other forms of evaluation, but it does have special importance in building confidence and credibility in the findings of cost-effectiveness and especially cost-benefit evaluations.

Sensitivity analysis is not confined to economic assessment; it is a basic concept of data analysis looking at how well a particular measure detects what it is intended to assess. In economic evaluations, it has particular value in providing for testing the effects on the overall analysis of making alternative assumptions, for example, about how to calculate costs for specific things. This is of special importance to those areas of cost or benefit estimation where judgements have to be made about resource use and consequences which are not otherwise apparent or clear.

For example, if staff training is to be included as a cost overhead (input) to running an evaluated programme, and where the same staff are also engaged in activities outside that programme, what proportion of the training costs should be allocated to the programme input costs? An assumption could be made (say 50%) but perhaps this could have an adverse and unfair effect on the overall staff costs. Sensitivity analysis allows for the evaluator to change that proportion to demonstrate what different assumptions (25%, 40%, 90%) might have on the overall cost-benefit calculation.

In economic evaluation there are two types of sensitivity analysis (Drummond et al, 2005) which can be used to test the vulnerability of the result to the assumptions and estimates in the analysis:

• One-way sensitivity analysis, which looks at different effects on the result by varying the values of each (selected) element in the analysis one at a time. Used like this, sensitivity analysis shows by just how much the assumed value of a cost or benefit would have to rise (for a cost) or fall (for a benefit) to 'tip' the cost-benefit finding from positive to negative. This will show how sensitive an analysis is to what might be small changes in the tested key elements.

• Multiway sensitivity analysis recognises that interrelationships between different costs and between costs and benefits are complex. This is usually tackled through scenario-based analysis, which typically involves the construction of a small range of alternative scenarios and conducting multiway sensitivity analysis within these to test for vulnerability of the cost-benefit analysis results to different circumstances. Scenarios need to be constructed according to the circumstances of what is being evaluated; typically this might be high, moderate and low demand scenarios; different labour market scenarios perhaps proxied by very low, low, moderate and high unemployment levels, or changes in overall economic circumstances.

One-way analysis is simpler, but may not be sophisticated enough where there is volatile demand or uncertainty over how different aspects affecting an intervention may interact.

Whichever pathway is taken, sensitivity analysis itself will need to make judgements about what assumptions to test, or what and how to shape testable scenarios. It cannot test for all possible alternatives or circumstances, so evaluators will need to make further assumptions about which cost or benefit factors, or circumstances, are the most likely to affect results or confidence in the overall analysis. Sensitivity analyses, and the rationale behind them, will be presented alongside the full cost-benefit evaluation to present alternative cost/benefit calculations. This will help position the robustness of the evaluation findings and build confidence in the results.

Avoiding pitfalls in economic evaluation

This chapter has shown how different pathways to economic evaluations approach the cost and value of inputs, outputs and outcomes in different ways. Choices need to be made early in the design process about which is appropriate to decision makers and their evidence needs. These choices need to be made very carefully and often start with what previous costs and benefits information or assumptions were made when it was decided to set up an intervention, policy or programme – its 'business case'. Without this, an economic evaluation risks producing information that may of itself be interesting, even challenging, but will be of little or no use to decision makers unless it fits with earlier assumptions or expectations of cost-benefits.

Searching questions also need to be asked when these choices are made. The more straightforward forms of economic evaluation, such as cost descriptions and cost minimisation analyses, may be within the scope of most competent evaluators, but cost-effectiveness evaluation and cost-benefit evaluation are likely to need higher levels of skill and understanding. So the next pitfall to avoid is making an overconfident judgement about whether those who are to conduct the evaluation are well-enough placed to do so.

To avoid other potential pitfalls, the following questions should be asked, before the choice is finalised:

- Is there clarity about the definition of what needs to be evaluated; are the boundaries and inclusions appropriate to give a full picture of costs (and consequences)?
- How narrowly defined are the inputs, outputs and outcomes?
- What allowances have been made for opportunity costs? Are these allowances appropriate; are they realistic?
- Has allowance also been made for the costs and consequences of non-intervention or inaction in the assessment?
- Will comparisons need to be made (for example, for cost minimisation, cost-effectiveness or cost avoidance), and if so, what is the rationale for selecting the comparators and what is their relevance and quality as benchmarks or alternative arrangements?

In many ways, good economic evaluation is more of an iterative process than other approaches, so evaluators also need to ask themselves (and continue to check out) if the assumptions made in selecting a full spectrum of (appropriate) costs, effects or benefits, and in monetising these, are appropriate. As part of this they will need to ask themselves:

- What is the rationale for the assumptions?
- Have these been fully shared and (for the final analysis) documented?
- What has been chosen to sensitivity test (and why), and has the alternative costs and benefits quantification arising been shared, including in the overall analysis?

These are not the only issues that might arise but asking these questions of those conducting an economic evaluation is likely to raise any other questions that might be more specific to the evaluation. Economic evaluation is often complex and will usually court some controversy, but taking account of the more common challenges and pitfalls should help to build the necessary confidence in and credibility of what is being done.

6

CONDUCTING IMPACT EVALUATION

- Outcomes, intermediate impacts and impacts – getting to grips with the jargon
- Understanding 'gross' and 'net' impacts, attribution and the counterfactual
- Use of randomised controlled trials, scope and limitations of fully experimental impact evaluation methods
- Partial or quasi-experimental methods as a practical impact measurement alternative
- Using non-experimental evaluation approaches to estimate impacts
- The use of qualitative approaches to assessing impact and contributions
- Avoiding pitfalls in impact evaluation

Introduction

Impact assessment has deep roots, but its increasing use in the social world, and relevance to public policy and decision-making, has seen an acceleration of new ideas and practice, especially in the last 20 years or so. The pace of these developments has not been easy to keep up with, and more than any other area of evaluation practice this has left a legacy of what may seem to be confusing and even contradictory approaches. Impact evaluation has consequently developed a special mystique, which can lead inexperienced evaluators to be cautious about what can, and cannot, be reliably measured or estimated. This chapter aims to uncloak some of the confusion that has arisen, explain the main methodological options and practical approaches now available, and set out their strengths and limitations. A good starting point is demystifying some of the jargon.

Unpicking the jargon

As Chapter 2 has shown, impact evaluation focuses on the *consequential changes* arising from an intervention. These are quite different from intervention outputs, which might be something delivered within the intervention, perhaps counselling or mentoring sessions, work trials, training, or developing new qualifications. These outputs are agents of change but not the change (impact) itself. A training course, for example, or even a qualification obtained at the end of it, does not of itself change someone's job situation, but securing a first or better job using that qualification – the impact – does. Other 'consequential changes' might be a school or college leaver making better-informed career or university choices, an unemployed participant securing a job, or a homeless person moving into secure accommodation.

These, and other impacts, are the real end product of whatever is being evaluated. They come in all shapes and sizes, depending on what is being evaluated, and present different challenges of measurement. All impact evaluations start with clarifying just what impacts are expected, and how to measure them – usually through setting impact measures or indicators. Here, a simple distinction is often made between 'hard' and 'soft' impact measures or indicators:

- A hard impact, such as placement in a new job for someone unemployed or non-offending behaviour following a post-custodial support programme, lends itself readily to precise definition and so to reliable quantification.

- Soft impacts, such as increased awareness or confidence in searching for a job, can be important in providing a more rounded picture of impacts but can be trickier to define and measure. They are often quantified by defining and using proxy measures, perhaps based on questionnaires to collect self-assessments (for example, of increased confidence).

While we have been referring here to impact evaluation to include both outcomes and impacts (as set out in Chapter 2) these are important distinctions for the impact evaluator. Both produce consequential changes, but outcomes refer to short- or medium-term changes and impacts to longer-term effects which may take some time to come about.

Some may refer to outcomes as 'intermediate impacts', but both are a consequential change apparent before a longer-term impact becomes apparent. For example, a novel programme of public health dietary advice to people with higher coronary risks might produce early measurable outcomes in lower blood pressure among participants, but might take some time before it could be expected to show impacts through reduced coronary incidences or extended lives.

The outcomes/impact distinction is a lot more than just semantics or the sequencing over time of measurable changes. In a world where funding cycles for new initiatives may be just two or three years (or less), where decision makers are looking for fast results, and speedy information to contribute to decision-making, it may not always be possible to quantify longer-term changes (impacts) within the life of an evaluation. All too often the focus of *impact* evaluation to meet decision makers' timetables can only be on early or intermediate changes, namely, outcomes. However, even here, good design will mean the methods chosen to measure outcomes will also provide for the indicators and measurement chain that any later evaluation could use to quantify longer-term changes.

A final point of jargon that can trip up the unprepared, is the distinction between direct and indirect impacts (and outcomes). Evaluators will have a pretty good idea of what the direct impacts will be – even if a logic chain (see Chapter 2) has not been put together, it is likely to be self-evident what main consequential changes are being aimed at by an intervention. However, not all of the impacts achieved may be anticipated; others may emerge as unexpected or knock-on effects – collectively referred to as 'indirect impacts'. You cannot measure what you don't know is there, but a carefully designed evaluation can help to identify unexpected impacts. Qualitative inputs, which include open questioning of beneficiaries, for example, are useful here and in a formative evaluation, and early identification may mean some remedial measurement can be put in place before the evaluation reaches a summative assessment. Being open to indirect benefits provides for a more robust view of all impact achievements – those expected and those not – and this can be very important to decision makers who may see added value in unexpected gains.

All this terminology is important. Evaluators may find themselves working with operational, policy or other staff, who may understand what is being evaluated and even what can (and cannot) be measured, but are not well versed in the jargon. As a result, evaluators may find themselves needing to unpick the jargon, and what it means for decision-making, to be confident they are working to realistic expectations. Using this terminology precisely and consistently with stakeholders and users is a cornerstone to effective impact evaluation.

Chasing the counterfactual

Providing counterfactual evidence is often the hardest of the evaluation principles for newcomers to evaluation to get their heads around. Impact evaluation is not just about defining and measuring what outcomes or impacts have occurred within an intervention; it needs to answer the almost inevitable question from users: 'To what extent were any measured effects due to what is being evaluated?' A young unemployed person may be recruited to a youth employability programme, attend regularly and get a job shortly afterwards; but is it clear that entry to that job was wholly due to the employability programme? Perhaps it came from an earlier job search which paid off later, a relative making overtures on their behalf, or a friend tipping them off about a likely vacancy. It may be easy to unpick this for a single individual, but to do so across a whole programme evaluators need to get to grips systematically with the *attribution* of measured impacts to the intervention activities.

This is where *counterfactual evidence* comes in, helping evaluators to understand what would have happened if the intervention had not taken place. With counterfactual evidence the evaluator's measurement of 'gross' impacts (that is, the total number of young people on the scheme subsequently securing jobs) can be discounted for what would otherwise have happened (that is, those who would have secured those jobs without the scheme) to assess 'net' impacts. Net impact is clearly a much more reliable measure of consequential change and the value secured from an intervention.

Looked at in this way it is not such a difficult idea to embrace; but it can be a tall order to determine how, and how reliably, you can measure, estimate or assess it. So, how do you measure or estimate what would have happened in the hypothetical event that the intervention had not taken place? Figure 6.1 summarises the three main recognised ways of quantifying counterfactual evidence.

These are the alternative approaches to demonstrating what would otherwise have happened in terms of impacts. How they are used is set out below. While they share a focus on quantification, they aim to answer slightly different questions and, if well designed, will generate different levels of confidence in their findings. So why the alternatives?

Many of those methods were developed first in health and medical interventions, where the situation for using what are called experimental impact evaluation methods – fully experimental randomised controlled trials (RCTs) or quasi (partially) experimental (QEs), for example – was favourable to collecting precise and comparable data sets in controlled or relatively stable environments. They are called experimental because the evaluator can anticipate the intervention and before it starts can set up, in effect, an experiment and study it, using principles and controls similar to those that might be used by a natural scientist in a laboratory.

Figure 6.1: Practical choices in measuring or estimating the counterfactual

Counterfactual approach	What is involved?	What question are evaluators seeking to answer?	Confidence and likely relative strength
Randomised controlled trial (RCT) Fully experimental	Outcome(s) is contrasted between a 'control' group and 'intervention' or treatment group, both being randomly selected and based either on individuals (I-RCT) or cluster groups (C-RCTs)	*To what extent does the intervention cause the observed outcome(s)?*	High
Quasi-experimental (QE) design Partially experimental	Contrasting intervention outcome(s) for participants in the intervention, with a closely matched but not randomised concurrent comparative group	*To what extent does the intervention have the expected outcome(s)?*	Moderately high
Non-experimental approach	Comparator evidence on outcomes is drawn from outside a designated group by using wider (often national) statistical sources manipulated to provide as close a comparison as possible to intervention participants	*To what extent does the intervention make a difference?*	Moderate to low

The real world is not a laboratory and clinical trials, on which policy-related RCTs are often modelled, and which usually take place in highly controlled situations, provide for more sophisticated design than is generally possible in a social setting. The stability and controls needed for such experimentation are often not achievable in the diverse and often complex contexts in which impact evaluators find themselves. Experimental impact evaluation consequently has its critics, notably among those emphasising a theory-based approach (Guba and Lincoln, 1989; Pawson and Tilley, 1997), and who doubt RCTs' practical value in social settings or question how well they provide for generalisable evidence. Set against this, in many advanced economies user expectations have continued to rise about the quantification of impact evaluation and the robustness needed for measuring 'net' impacts taking account of the counterfactual. On some occasions governments have seemingly recommended the use of experimental methods in circumstances that may be beyond their usual scope (Haynes et al, 2012).

This juxtaposition of criticism from some evaluation theorists, with rising and sometimes often unrealistic expectations from users to use RCTs, confuses even experienced evaluators about the relative merits of experimental approaches. But this is not a question of either/or – which some theorists seem to suggest. In fact, there is no universal approach that can fit the many and complex circumstances of impact evaluation in respect of vastly different initiatives. The real dilemma is in how best to choose and fit existing available approaches or variants of them to needs and circumstances. This dilemma needs to be tackled for each evaluation, individually and separately, and to do so evaluators need to be well-enough versed in the attributes of the main pathways, each of which is looked at below.

Fully experimental methods and RCTs

A well-designed RCT is the gold standard for providing counterfactual evidence in an impact evaluation. However, the bar for an RCT design is set high. First and foremost, interventions need to have anticipated the need for an RCT (or QE) and will be a non-starter if this was not thought about after until the intervention has started –a situation facing evaluators far too often. Even where it is anticipated, designers need to be hyper-cautious about avoiding flaws in randomisation (in the intervention and control groups) or constraints in the management of the trial. For RCTs, 'good enough is not good enough'.

Most readers are not likely to face a situation where they will be able to harness the strong counterfactual potential of an RCT; but it remains important to understand where and when they are (and are not) well fitted, especially in managing the expectations of clients who may be less well versed in the practical realities. Reduced to its essence, conducting an RCT that inspires confidence (and credibility) in its design, needs:

- recruitment of an appropriate large group of participating people, or other unit of evaluation (for example, businesses), that are relevant to measuring the outcome that the intervention is intended to produce;
- division of these based on *probability methods* into two groups – an intervention (or treatment) group and a control group – with assignment to groups by randomised selection to ensure that one group mirrors the other in its diverse characteristics;
- introduction and management of the intervention to the assigned groups over an appropriate timeframe, using agreed protocols for consistency of implementation and to ensure influences (beyond the intervention itself) that might affect outcomes or impacts are minimised (and where they occur are identified and adjusted for in the analysis);
- uniformly collected (and analysed) appropriate outcomes and impact indicator evidence and conditioning data to statistically contrast (and validate) the different effects for the intervention and non-intervention groups.

There are different ways to classify RCTs but the two most common involve either a *parallel group* approach where participants are randomly assigned to the intervention or control group, and where all in each group receive, or do not receive, the intervention; or a *crossover* design where, over time, each participant receives (or does not receive) an intervention in a random sequence. Crossover groups can be useful for managing ethical compliance but in practice (and along with other study designs) are rare outside some medical trials.

A more significant distinction for RCTs in the social world is between groups based on individual participants – *individual-level randomised controlled trials* (I-RCTs) – or 'clusters' of participants – *cluster randomised controlled trials* (C-RCTs). For example, a trial of a new vocational skills assessment method may see individual college students assigned directly on a randomised basis to the treatment or control group, where both intervention and control protocols and data are administered in an individual setting (an I-RCT). However, it may be more suitable for the trial and data to be collected by tutor or class groups (not individuals) and here clusters of students (for example, whole classes) are randomised (a C-RCT). It is also possible to combine the two approaches, with clustered data collected in the intervention group and individual data in the control group.

Cluster approaches are often used in education settings where it would be impractical to secure informed consent (from non-adults) and where data may be more easily collected in class groups. Example 9 below shows the use of a C-RCT in assessing the impact of a free breakfast initiative in primary schools.

Example 9: Using a cluster-RCT to evaluate the primary school free breakfast initiative

Research shows one of the causes of poorer achievements, and classroom disruption among 5–11 year-old pupils from more deprived backgrounds is the nutritional effects of breakfast-skipping at home. In 2007, the Welsh Assembly Government (in the UK) started a trial of a free healthy breakfasts programme for primary schools in Wales. All primary schools in Wales were given the opportunity to participate and more than 1,000 schools took part. A cluster randomised controlled trial was set up in parallel, with an embedded process evaluation, to assess the (net) impact of providing free breakfasts in schools on children's eating habits, quality of nutrition, cognitive functioning and classroom behaviour.

The C-RCT design was chosen because the programme was implemented at the whole school level and randomisation for individual pupils was not possible. The cluster approach recruited 111 primary schools; 56 randomly assigned to the 'control' group and 55 to the intervention. The C-RCT involved 4,350 pupils based on one Year 5 (9–10 years) and one Year 6 (10–11 years) cluster randomly selected as the data collection unit in each school. Baseline (start) data were collected for these (for each school) and then again 4 and 12 months after.

The C-RCT showed positive and statistically validated net impacts for the scheme as a dietary intervention with strong take-up among pupils in intervention schools, better nutrition among pupils, and more positive pupil attitudes towards breakfast. However, there was no significant effect on measured episodic memory or classroom inattention. The evaluation concluded that the lack of a significant effect on cognitive functioning and classroom behaviour reflected the C-RCT design and suggested that tracking change at the individual level (not possible in the C-RCT design) might have produced evidence of a more positive effect.

(For more, see Murphy et al, 2007)

While I-RCTs are not commonplace outside medical and health trials, they are more widespread than C-RCTs. I-RCTs can be organised as *blinded* RCTs, where the people in, and managing, intervention (treatment) and control (placebo) groups know they are in a trial (the RCT would risk being unethical if not) but not which of the two groups they are in; or as *non-blinded* RCTs, where individuals do know. Blinding provides for a higher level of control on the counterfactual analysis and where the trial will be strictly managed and monitored to ensure that nothing else (other than the intervention) that might have a bearing on the outcomes does so. Distinctions have been made between single, double and even triple-blinded RCTs but the latest Consolidated Standards of Reporting Trials (CONSORT) guidelines have discredited these as practical differences (Schulz et al (2010); the only real difference is if a trial is blinded or not.

Other variants of RCTs also exist (Shadish et al, 2002), but whatever approach is taken to randomisation, and controlled circumstances, the duration and size of an RCT will also matter. An RCT needs to be of a duration in which an observable outcome or impact can be expected to be apparent. A psychotherapy behaviour improvement programme for longer sentence offenders in custody cannot expect a combination of counselling, peer mentoring and professional support to produce observable impacts to deep-seated behaviours in a few weeks. An RCT in such a case might need a year or longer to see even early outcomes.

An experimental approach such as an RCT needs an appropriate number of units (for example, participants) in the control and intervention groups to provide robust results. Here, the size of the trial will need to anticipate how much 'net' impact might be expected. Researchers looking at the US, Canada and the UK have shown that the effects of government-funded social programmes are often modest (Government Social Research Unit, 2007) so sample sizes might need to be large to detect net outcomes that are reliable. Trial size may also depend on what is needed of the analysis, so if an offender psychotherapeutic trial wanted to contrast results for types of offender institutions, age groups or types of offence, it would need viable numbers in each subgrouping in both the intervention and control groups.

These are all essential requirements for conducting an RCT. For many evaluation circumstances in social settings these often add up to a tall order, and RCTs could be said to be 'contraindicated' where:

- the level of resource available to the evaluation, or the skill-mix in the evaluation team, cannot meet the exacting demands of RCT design, management and analysis;
- the intervention is small-scale and the (considerable) costs of an RCT cannot be justified;
- the budget or time available is not consistent with anticipated 'net' impacts (larger sample sizes) and/or observable effects (viable duration);

- randomisation requirements cannot be supported by the information available on the people or units to be assigned, or where that information is inaccurate or incomplete;
- ethical considerations make RCTs impossible, for example, where informed consent to participate cannot be assured or where randomisation might risk harm to those in a control group (see Chapter 3 for ethical controls);
- an intervention has already been running for some time, and where it will probably be impossible to control for influences from past practices and participant expectations;
- an intervention involves multiple actions (which might variously affect outcomes) or in a complex environment with many confounding variables that cannot be controlled for or statistically isolated;
- there is a significant risk to the likely integrity of the RCT, such as different dropout (attrition) rates between intervention and control groups, or the likelihood of participant behavioural bias, sometimes referred to as the Hawthorne effect (see Example 10 below).

In most social situations, RCTs will be more suited for quantifiable testing of new and limited-aim initiatives at pilot or pre-scale up stages. However, in applying an RCT evaluators face many challenges, and RCTs are not a likely evaluation tool for most of the circumstances in which evaluators find themselves. Where this is the case, and where users still require a high level of certainty or generalisability in the findings, evaluators may need to work with users and other stakeholders to manage (down) expectations (see Chapter 2).

Example 10: Taking account of participation behavioural bias – the Hawthorne effect

The Hawthorne effect is named after an early use of experimental methods outside of medicine. This is a classic illustration of how RCTs need to take account of confounding factors, in this case, behavioural effects on the measured 'net' impacts. The RCT involved a series of experiments at the Western Electric Company's US plant at Hawthorne, Chicago, in the late 1920s and early 1930s. These explored productivity impacts of changes to physical workplace environments, with the evaluation team led by Elton Mayo, later professor of industrial research at Harvard. Each experiment used an implementation and control group of assigned workers.

Across a series of RCTs (investigating the effects of raised shop floor lighting levels, changed shifts/working hours, changed sequencing and duration of rest breaks) the evaluation team found that the productivity of the employees in the intervention group showed significant net increases over that of the control group. However, the evaluation also showed contradictions, such as when productivity improved when the lights were dimmed. By the time the trials had concluded, productivity at the plant was at its highest level. Other impact measures also showed positive changes such as a sharp fall in absenteeism.

The trials had inadvertently demonstrated the need to control for confounding variables in RCTs, in this case the behavioural influences on all workers, where further analysis (much later) showed the major effect on productivity had not been the changes in specific working conditions but the influences on motivation and morale resulting from the sense among workers that someone was actually concerned about their workplace conditions, and was engaging them in the process. Since the 1950s the need for experimental evaluation methods to set the individual in a social context and to allow for confounding factors such as behavioural influences has been known as the Hawthorn effect.

For further information on the Hawthorne trials see: Gillespie G (1991).

Quasi-experimental methods

If an RCT is not possible, experimental principles can still be used through *quasi-experimental* (QE) methods. These may be well-suited when randomisation or strict management of implementation and control groups are not possible. Ideas about QE methods have been developing in the 50 years since their potential for social policy research was first suggested (Campbell and Stanley, 1966). Different views have since emerged about what constitutes a quasi-experimental design, but they share the common feature of setting a (non-randomised) comparison group against an intervention group. These *concurrent comparison groups are* a mainstay of quasi-experimental designs, and can be applied in different ways, for example:

- A pre-participation group – often useful where the evaluated policy or initiative is to be phased in over different times or in 'waves' and not simultaneously everywhere. A pre-participation comparative group will be one of the areas to be assigned to later waves, and is suitable where expected outcomes occur on a relatively short timescale (that is, before the comparison joins rollout), and where whatever is being implemented does not change over time.
- Matched (geographical) areas – where a comparison to a pilot area may be picked to very closely match the socioeconomic or other relevant characteristics of the intervention area. This is a common QE method and is stronger when not relying on a single comparator group (Cook and Campbell, 1979). Comparative areas are not likely to be adjacent otherwise they might be affected by *leakage* or *substitution* of actions from the intervention group to the comparison. Difference in statistical analyses can pick out the 'net impacts' from outcomes between the intervention and outcome groups (Example 3 in Chapter 3 provides an example of this approach).
- Intermittent application – where evaluators may find themselves asked to assess the impacts of interventions that involve short-

term but intermittent phases of activity, perhaps applied at different times in different areas or target markets (for example, area-based promotional campaigns linked to public policy initiatives). Where different areas receive these interventions at different times, QE methods might choose 'quiet' areas at a specific point in time to contrast with active areas.

• Opt in/opt out approaches – where potential participants who choose not to be involved in the intervention group can be used as the basis of a comparison group. So if the evaluation in Example 7 could not use its C-RCT design it might have used an 'opt out' comparison group of schools drawn from those who decided not to take part in the free breakfast programme. This requires careful matching of the two groups on key characteristics to minimise selection biases and to control for other potentially distorting influences on outcomes such as motivations.

• Administrative or eligibility boundaries – where a comparison might be selected from, for example, an age or status group not eligible to take part in the intervention but very close in its characteristics. A pre-release offender behavioural programme focused on reducing impulsivity in nonviolent offenders and centred on those serving sentences of under three years and within six months of release, might be working with all in scope (and so not have a direct comparator) but could select as a comparison nonviolent offenders within six months of release serving slightly longer sentences of 36–48 months.

• Parallel modalities – which will select a concurrent comparison group from another intervention where the actions have very similar goals (and will be measuring some of the same outcomes) but different modalities. For example, a programme might be applied across different areas and where different partners (for example, local governments and councils) may have some discretion on use of funding or how the intervention is implemented locally. Here, it may be possible to classify different areas according to these differences, and to contrast outcomes for areas with extended funding or activities with a comparator area or areas implementing the basic policy to show impact effects from variants of the policy.

The strongest QE designs will probably be pre-participation groups and matched areas, but most of these approaches rely for their strength on the quality of matching of the intervention and comparative groups to maximise the internal validity. This aims to get a comparative sample as close as possible in its features to the intervention group, such as a comparative area where socioeconomic and demographic factors showed very similar population characteristics and levels of deprivation. Project Bernie, for example, which we saw in Example 3 (Chapter 3), used a QE design based on a selecting Aberdare as a concurrent matched geographical comparison to the Tonypandy pilot area, harnessing a range of local authority data to select a close-fit comparator.

Good QE design also needs to 'match' by smoothing out other possible biases that might make the evaluated outcomes more or less likely, and where judgement alone may not be enough to show 'closeness'. Here, evaluators (supported by statisticians) can use propensity statistical methods to help 'match' comparative groups. Propensity score matching (PSM) is a common method, but inverse probability treatment weighting (IPTW) methods have also been used in the medical evaluation sphere and may be better when working with small samples (Pirracchio et al, 2012).

These are not the only QE options, but they are the most common. Others can be applied in some circumstances, such as matched-pair contrasts for small-scale (small-n) evaluations (see Chapter 3), or longitudinal self-controlled evaluations and retrospective case control evaluations, which have often been used in medical and health situations (Ovretveit, 1997). QE methods have scope for more creative design, than the rigid requirements of RCTs, but with this flexibility comes the responsibility of evaluators choosing and designing what is most effective for a particular case. All QE approaches lack the strength and confidence of a well-designed RCT. However, they will not be harnessed as substitutes but as alternatives where an RCT is not viable, and a well-chosen QE approach can be a good second-best choice.

A useful way of testing the likely strength of a proposed QE approach is the Maryland Scale. It was first developed by researchers at the University of Maryland working specifically within the US criminal justice and crime prevention system (Sherman et al, 1997). Professor Sherman and his team developed a five-point scale to critically assess levels of QE rigour and likely validity on impact evaluation approaches. The Maryland Scientific Methods Scale (SMS) provides a framework to evaluate the methodological quality of approaches in much wider areas of social policy and beyond the United States.

Experimental methods of impact evaluation – RCTs and QE – can be good at measuring net impacts by providing the necessary counterfactual evidence of what would otherwise have happened if the intervention had not taken place. They can be robust, and credible to users and stakeholders who may not understand the complexities needed in RCT or QE design but will see how the control or comparative group evidence can be used to calculate 'net' impacts. What they do not readily provide is much understanding of how or why interventions, or aspects of them, bring about change. These 'hows' and 'whys' may be very important for decision makers looking to build on evaluation evidence to improve interventions.

Unfortunately, the requirements for experimental methods mean it is methodologically challenging for an RCT or QE approach to add in other evidence collection methods to look at the 'hows' and 'whys' without the risk of distorting the results. Fully experimental designs have been criticised for this limitation, sometimes harshly, with some evaluation theorists consequently doubting their utility in most social contexts (Pawson and Tilley, 1997). It is in fact challenging but not impossible to use hybrid methods in fully experimental designs. Some of these constraints can be overcome by conducting case studies, interviews or deliberative methods ahead of an RCT (but not of participants who will later be in the implementation or control groups, or in some way associated with them). Or these might be conducted afterwards with follow-up interviews 'nested' in the evaluation design but conducted in such a way as not to interfere with it. This is one way of combining qualitative insights with the quantitative core of an RCT, although adding to costs and possibly timescales. For QE approaches, combining qualitative methods is much less problematic.

There is plenty of choice in experimental designs; the challenge is finding what is viable in different circumstances and in relation to different needs. To help with this, some of the main influences are brought together in a ready reckoner to review, for the four considerations most likely to affect evaluators in deciding when RCTs/ QEs are more or less viable, namely:

- resource availability
- the nature of what is being evaluated
- the scale of likely impacts(s)
- access to likely data
- Likely potential for comparators data.

This is set out in Annex B.

Non-experimental evaluation

An RCT may be the so-called gold standard and a QE approach a close second, but often these will not be feasible or desirable and evaluators will find themselves looking instead at non-experimental methods. These are a third-best choice and are sometimes called *constrained designs* but do go some way towards counterfactual analysis. They do not have a control or comparator group, and have no experimental protocols, but instead use parallel data to estimate what would otherwise have happened in the absence of the intervention.

Using non-experimental approaches is not liked by many, and some have come close to dismissing their use as having limited value to decision-makers (HM Treasury, 2011). They lack the strength and credibility of a well-designed RCT or QE impact evaluation, and have no place as cost-saving substitutes. However, where fully or partially experimental methods are just not possible, they can have a role to play in providing quantitative evidence to estimate 'net' impacts. Some of the ways this can be done are:

- Benchmark statistical comparisons: If suitable data are available it may be possible to estimate 'what would otherwise have happened' from official or other data sources or surveys. For example, an intervention aimed at boosting export performance in small and medium-sized enterprises (SMEs), might contrast data from the evaluated activity to what 'all firms' nationally were doing by tapping existing government (federal) business surveys so as to estimate net impacts. All benchmark data needs to be appropriate, involving the same or a very similar 'population' and outcomes data for comparison if and where this is available and where it is appropriately classified.

- 'Before and after' analysis: This will be an option for nearly all evaluations, drawing on comparisons within the intervention group itself, taking data at the start of an intervention (for those taking part) and the same data at the end of the scheme of participation (or at some key point afterwards) as a pre-and post-test methodology. This readily shows the gross impact, and may be able to control for some other variables that could also have affected the outcome. Before and after analysis will always be open to the criticism that unknown influences or *confounding variables* outside the intervention influenced some of the change, and these designs are best suited to when what is evaluated is so straightforward that the intervention is the only thing reasonably expected to influence the result.

- Trajectory analysis: This is a form of time series analysis using pre-implementation (historic) data, where it is available, to estimate net impacts by comparing achieved outcomes in the intervention with the projected outcome over the same time, perhaps using linear extrapolation. Obviously this needs suitable historic outcome data, limited (or disaggregated) to the target group, and which is sufficiently robust for extrapolation. It also needs to take into account possible disturbances (for example, changes in markets, economic or other conditions). As with before-and-after analysis, the constraint is that all things are not usually equal and the analysts will need to use often sophisticated methods to try to discount any such effects.

- Non-matched outcome contrasts: It is often possible to set the (gross) outcomes achieved from an intervention against the same indicators from 'non-matched' comparator groups. Typically this involves administrative or geographical areas of the same status as the implementation area, but it could also contrast parts of the economy or sectors. Taken at face value this is a poor comparison because there is no attempt to match comparisons to exclude selection or influencing bias. However, where multiple non-matched comparators are used, this may provide a series of benchmarks to contrast the intervention achievements against similar situations where the intervention did not take place.

Unlike experimental methods, these approaches can be used together, perhaps combining (where the data can provide for it) a whole population benchmark and a before and after analysis or trajectory analysis. Each will probably provide a different estimate of net effects (by using different methods) but this can be used as a basis for reporting higher and lower net impact ranges in the evaluation. Example 11 shows a business support programme evaluation which was able to combine non-experimental methods in its impact evaluation.

Example 11: Non experimental impact evaluation of a business support network

A sub-regional small business support initiative was set up by two UK universities working together to test and facilitate university-to-business innovation and performance groups. This involved a number of facilitated small groups of small and micro-businesses, and some recent start-ups, working in high-value sectors. Following a trial, it was rolled out to membership and eventually over 1,000 firms had been members of these subsidised groups, typically for three years each, with expert facilitators supporting self-determined agendas for business-to-business learning. By 2010 the programme was funded by six different national, regional and local government and other agencies.

6. CONDUCTING IMPACT EVALUATION

With the programme nearing the end of its funding period in 2012, programme managers decided that a more substantial impact evaluation would be needed to demonstrate the added value and return on investment of the business support model, and to also support bids for further funding. Extensive in-programme monitoring information was available on member firms, and with too little time available to set up a quasi-experimental design, managers decided on a non-experimental impact evaluation using these data. Recognising the limitations on relying on any single non-experimental approach, the impact evaluation developed a twin-stranded impact analysis to provide comparative data:

- A contrast of participant firms with geographically disaggregated 'all firms' data for two key performance measures for SMEs: annual profit before tax and overall turnover levels. The indicators were chosen because they were generic and could apply across all business circumstances as broad measures of business. Comparative data came from disaggregating national data sets to provide sub-regional comparative data for the project area.
- A before and after analysis limited to the member firms who had retained involvement with the allocated support group for at least two years and using a wider range of business improvement metrics drawn from programme monitoring data. A trajectory analysis was also considered but abandoned because there was too little pre-project historic data and because it would exclude new start-up members.

Using the nationally disaggregated data, the evaluation was able to show rising benefits with net gains from member firms averaging +1.3% for gross profit (before tax) and +6.7% for turnover, substantially outperforming non-members' profits over the same time period of -15.2% and +3.2 respectively. The management information also showed substantial improvements for members, including increased pre-recession turnover (+19% pa), improved strategies for business planning, innovation and collaboration, and an increase of 37% in business-to-business collaborations and joint ventures.

Whichever non-experimental approach (or combination) is adopted, it will be especially important to pay attention to the effects of unintended consequences of what is being evaluated – 'deadweight' effects, substitution or leakage (see Figure 6.2). This may require additional evidence gathering to assess these effects and to set them against whatever outcomes and impacts have been assessed.

Figure 6.2: Allowing for unintended consequences

Unintended consequence	Definition
Displacement	Positive outcomes are offset by a negative outcome of the same intervention, programme or policy elsewhere
Substitution	The participation effects and benefits on an individual, group or area are realised at the expense of other groups
Leakage	Benefits from the intervention which fall to others outside the funded scope, target area or group
Deadweight	Supports outcomes which would have happened anyway without the intervention taking place
Additionality	The net changes, outcomes or impacts over and above what was expected

Where appropriate comparative data is available, this may be manipulated to intensify its internal validity (see Chapter 7) and to provide for rapid evidence and analysis, at low (and perhaps no) additional costs and with few, if any, of the ethical considerations and risks that need be taken into account for RCTs or QE designs. As in Example 10, if an intervention has already started, where users have come late to realising they need an impact evaluation, or where a staged or formative review of outcomes is needed, non-experimental methods may be the only pathways open to evaluators.

The great disadvantage of non-experimental methods is that they can only provide estimates of what would otherwise have happened.

Quantification of net impacts based on this will be (much) less reliable, but if the expected net outcomes are large these methods may be sufficient to meet decision makers' needs. Where they are used, the limitations of non-experimental designs need to be transparent, and well-rehearsed in reporting. These are called constrained designs for good reason, but in some circumstances they remain a legitimate approach and, if appropriately analysed, may be able to provide sufficient evidence to guide decision makers on the added value from outcomes (or lack of it).

Qualitative methods and assessing impact

We have already seen that qualitative methods, including post-participation interviews and case studies, can help quantitative impact evaluations go beyond measurement of impacts, to provide evidence of how and why interventions work (or could work better). These 'nested' methodologies need very careful design and timing (especially for RCTs) but for other impact evaluations qualitative methods have real strength when used in combination with quantitative evidence. Sometimes they may even stand centre stage in an evaluation, although it is doubtful if an impact evaluation wholly based on qualitative methods would attract sufficient confidence or credibility in the value, and especially generalisability, of outcomes evidence.

In recent years there has been growing interest in and enthusiasm for the use of qualitative methods, frequently stemming from a different way of looking at causation in the more complex social contexts that often face impact evaluators. Aligned to ideas of 'generative causation', they look to explain what and why different influencing factors as a whole bring about the expected outcomes. A particularly influential focus has been the use of *realistic evaluation* designs (Pawson and Tilley, 1997) as an alternative to non-empirical approaches. These have captured the imagination of many, and have seen wide use, although there have been various interpretations of how best to use such methods to identify and assess context and mechanisms in realising outcomes (Marchal et al, 2012).

Whether following sophisticated realistic evaluation approaches or other orientations, qualitative approaches to impact evaluation do not measure or estimate attribution of impacts (and may philosophically avoid doing so) but they can go some way to assessing the likely quality of effects, and how these came about. Readers will mostly be well versed in the diversity of qualitative methods that could contribute (for example, case studies, beneficiary interviews), and their pros and cons, so these are not revisited here. Instead, three particular ways that qualitative designs can contribute to impact evaluation are looked at here:

- qualitative comparative analysis
- contribution analysis
- generative case studies.

Qualitative comparative analysis

Qualitative comparative analysis (QCA) is a theory-driven (*set theoretic*) approach, especially useful with small-n evaluations (see Chapter 3). It provides a very precise way of qualitatively analysing case-based (and similar) evidence of how different aspects of an intervention influence outcomes. As with the other qualitative approaches looked at here, it can use combinations of both quantitative and qualitative evidence to unpick often complex forms of causation in different contexts. Although typically used with small subsets of evidence, there is a need to have enough cases to demonstrate the different associations likely to affect an outcome. However, these may not need to be very numerous; QCA originator, Charles Ragin, put this as typically 5–50 cases:

> In this range, there are often too many cases for researchers to keep all the case knowledge 'in their heads,' but too few cases for most conventional statistical techniques. (Ragin, 2000, p 44)

The precise method (not considered here) needs careful application, but is well mapped elsewhere with evaluators in mind (Schneider and Wagemann, 2012; Schatz and Welle, 2016).

Contribution analysis

Contribution analysis (CA) as developed by John Mayne (Mayne, 2001) owes a lot to 'realistic evaluation' (Pawson and Tilley, 1997). CA originated from concerns about the practical limitations for policy makers of experimental approaches to outcome or impact attribution. Working with existing quantitative and qualitative evidence, it provides a way of strengthening and critically reviewing evidence to see how much of the success (or failure) of a programme can be attributed to its focus or to other influences – its *contribution*. CA qualitatively assesses the quality of attribution of measured impacts using six steps:

- Step 1: Develop the results chain (using and refining existing evidence)
- Step 2: Assess the existing evidence on results
- Step 3: Assess the alternative explanations
- Step 4: Assemble the 'results' narrative (the 'performance story')
- Step 5: Seek out, test and strengthen (additional) evidence on causal explanations
- Step 6: Revise and strengthen the performance story.

The 'strengthening techniques' of step 5 are important, and include deliberative methods and critical review by 'knowledgeable others', which can also help to raise the external credibility of the analysis. Although yet to be widely used, the approach has more flexibility than QCA and has been set out in detail in Mayne's early and subsequent publications (Mayne and Rist, 2006) and others (Scottish Government, 2011).

Generative case studies

Case studies, as a deep evidence-gathering and analytical technique, will be well known to social researchers and others, and are a common part of process and small-n evaluations (Byrne, 2009). Their use in impact evaluation is more likely to follow either generative approaches to understanding causation or the idea of *multiple causation* (Byrne, 2009; Stern et al, 2012) but they may also be used as a complementary nested method within experimental methods. Two approaches to exploring causal relationships are of particular value:

- tracking forward case studies
- tracking back case studies.

Tracking forward cases have been more common and can focus on either a part of an intervention, a specific activity or provider, or participants, as individuals or in groups. Typically, they draw on a combination of documentary, primary and secondary evidence (which may well include in-programme quantitative or survey information), often to progressively review the experiences and reflections of researchers and users. The output is a single impact case study, although in evaluations several cases are likely to be developed in parallel to provide for either a cross-section of experience, themed selections or a focus on better practice. This can also be applied retrospectively, although with challenges of rationalisation and access. Progressive and retrospective case studies *track forward* the achievement of outcomes, and from the start of the intervention, with outcomes and impacts identified, set in context and identifying influencing factors to provide a summative assessment (end of intervention or post-intervention) of the quality of attribution of outcomes to the intervention.

Tracking back case studies have a different emphasis, and can be (much) more resource intensive. They have been used much less commonly than tracking forward cases and are more likely to centre on a single targeted 'case'. These track back a specific and identified ex post outcome to review its historic development and contributions, both from the intervention and from other causes. The method starts with an existing and identified effect, although with uncertain attribution, for example an ex-offender resettlement programme known to have resulted in higher levels of early offender employment, but where the contribution of non-programme influences was not known. This approach can provide rich understanding of impact processes, determinants and influences. Its weakness is in the risks of rationalisation and the length of the period examined necessarily meaning that contact may have been lost with participants, key staff in providers, stakeholders and others (who may have moved on).

Tracking back and tracking forward approaches can be combined in hybrid studies (Parsons et al, 2014) to show causality or attribution in impact evaluation where the intervention contexts are diverse but broadly comparable. Although falling short of quantified causal analysis, these two case study approaches can provide valuable, if not comprehensive, evidence of influencing processes and illustrations of effects. They have particular value to small-n evaluations (White and Philips, 2012), but also as alternative or complementary methods to larger-scale impact evaluation. Whatever the context, and as with QCA and QA, they can help to assess counterfactual evidence but do not measure or estimate it. While they lack the robustness of quantification, they have the benefit of providing evidence that can put a face to impacts and influencing processes in terms of what they look like in practice. Experience shows that such illustrations can have a persuasive effect on decision makers, especially when combined with other, often quantitative evidence across the intervention.

Avoiding pitfalls in impact evaluation

Evaluation theorists have taken a particular interest in impact evaluation, with different, sometimes confusing, alternatives for how the issues of measurement, understanding, attribution and causality should be approached. This chapter has only scratched the surface of explaining the conceptual foundations of these alternatives, which are more fully described elsewhere (Fox et al, 2016). Instead, it has opted to cut across what may seem apparently competitive alternatives to look at what approaches – experimental, non-experimental and alternative – can help evaluators to avoid perhaps the greatest pitfall: the risk of making poorly founded or ill-advised design choices.

Choosing the 'right' design needs an understanding of these alternatives, but it is about much more than a technical choice. A starting point is to develop a common understanding between evaluators, commissioners and users, of what impact evidence or focus is necessary, and what methods are viable, proportionate and appropriate for particular decision-making needs. This may mean taking a step back to look again at expectations and priorities, with one of the early exponents of experimental approaches in social contexts later reflecting that making design choices means some trade-offs are inevitable:

> … we think it unrealistic to expect that a single piece of research will effectively answer all of the validity questions surrounding even the simplest causal relationship. (Cook and Campbell, 1979, p 83)

Commissioners or users are not likely to start this process, so it is often down to evaluators to kick-start it by looking in particular at the following questions:

- Has an appropriate methodological balance been achieved between the need to inform decision-making about the impact of the intervention itself, set against informing decisions about wider application or generalisability of evidence?
- Is the choice of methodology determined mainly by budgetary or time constraints? If so, what are the consequences for the confidence and credibility of the impact assessment (and quality of attribution); have users understood and endorsed these?
- Is there clarity about what context and outcomes are being evaluated and is this reflected in the outcome and impact

indicator(s) proposed? Is the evaluation timeframe appropriate for meeting those expectations?

- Is the evaluation centred on measuring a single anticipated outcome or impact (for which an RCT might be suitable) or do expectations mean that there is a need to assess several (including, perhaps, indirect effects)? If multiple outcomes or impacts are being considered, are these appropriately anticipated (are there significant others?) and do these cover an appropriate mix of hard and soft, direct and indirect outcomes and impacts?
- Is the evaluation timetable appropriate for the lead times needed to review (longer-term) impacts? If the focus is wholly on early or intermediate outcomes, is there scope to also build in evidence capture that can provide for subsequent impact measurement, and if not have user expectations been managed to recognise this as a future constraint?
- If an RCT is chosen, is there sufficient confidence that the quality of randomisation and control, as well as the evaluation scale and duration, are appropriate? If not, what can be done to strengthen the approach to avoid selection or implementation bias?
- If a QE approach is being adopted, is there confidence that the proposed comparator(s) selections and quality of matching, fit the evaluation circumstances and needs? Have leakage or substitution risks been avoided or allowed for?
- For either an RCT or QE, can the appropriateness of the choices (using the ready reckoner in Annex B) and their relative strength be demonstrated through peer review or perhaps using the Maryland Scale?
- If neither an RCT nor QE is possible (or appropriate) and a constrained design is being used, have the limitations been rehearsed with users, and is it possible to make these clear in the reporting? Has an allowance been made for an assessment of unintended consequences in any estimation of outcomes and impacts?

Asking these questions helps to build the necessary mutual understanding of what is being planned, and may mean realigning expectations of what the evaluation design can do. This takes time – time that may be under pressure for intensive impact evaluations – but this process should mean that future pitfalls can be minimised and often avoided altogether.

7

ANALYSIS, REPORTING AND COMMUNICATIONS

- The role of reporting and maximising the opportunities for use of evaluation evidence
- Choosing the most appropriate deliverables and evaluation outputs
- Demonstrating reliability and validity of the evaluation evidence
- Building confidence and credibility in the evaluation; handling negative findings
- Going beyond reporting and harnessing wider approaches to communications

Introduction

Evaluation evidence does not speak for itself. Its end point is usually seen as some form of summative reporting, often in a combination of written and oral reporting. Doing this effectively involves juggling the competing demands of sifting and condensing a multiplicity of evidence, with the necessary health warnings, and producing a narrative that is readily understood by (and useful to) decision makers. This can be quite a balancing act, but providing for 'good' reporting goes much further if the value of evaluation findings for decision-making are to be maximised. This chapter looks also at some of those parallel needs and how evaluators can play an active role in building both confidence in the evidence and its credibility.

Reporting and informing decision-making

Evaluation evidence is rarely the sole influence on users. Even evidence-based policy (and practice) is rarely guided wholly by evaluation, research or systematic evidence. Figure 7.1 shows that decision makers are subject to multiple influences. Most of these are not evidence-based, so the odds are often stacked against evaluators' evidence playing a leading role.

Figure 7.1: Influencing change

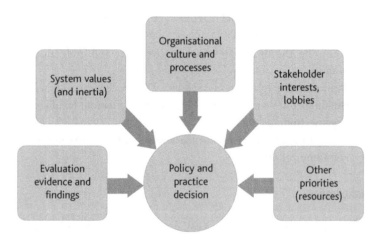

To improve these odds, and to start to raise the profile of evidence in decision-making, evaluators need to go further than end reporting and play an active role in helping users to unpick the evidence and its implications. This is not a universally accepted idea. Even within the evaluation community, some see their role ending with a signed-off report, placing the emphasis on users putting all the effort into appreciating the implications of the evidence in their decision-making. Users may also endorse this narrow perspective and feel more comfortable with the evaluation role ending with factual reporting. However, my own experience as a user and evaluator shows 'reporting' responsibilities often need to go the extra mile if the evaluation evidence is to be used effectively. For me, the evaluator has a 'duty of care' in helping to maximise the use and value of evaluation findings for those decision-makers, although this will always fall short of an active role in making those decisions.

At a minimum, this duty of care needs evaluators to provide a user-orientated and comprehensible assessment of evaluation findings and implications, and this may involve more than one reporting product to reach different user groupings. Few evaluators would disagree with this, although views may differ as to what constitutes 'user-orientated' reporting. Yet there is scope, and often need, for the evaluator to go much further.

In the policy arena, and often elsewhere, evidence needs exploring and unpicking to be readily understood by those influencing and informing decision makers. Users understand policies and their ambition, priorities, and the context for decision-taking, but the evaluator is best placed to understand what the evidence is saying, its strengths and limitations. Effective use of evaluations consequently often needs pre- and post-reporting collaboration between user and evaluator to avoid the real risks that evidence will be neglected or misinterpreted.

Such a collaboration may not suit all circumstances, and the opportunities for maximising the use of the evaluation evidence consequently vary, in particular in:

- the context of what is being evaluated and decision-making needs;
- the type of the evaluation conducted;
- users' specified needs for deliverables and dissemination.

Evaluation and decision-making context

At its heart, the relationship between evaluation and decision-making is about how systematic evidence is mobilised. There have been different attempts to codify evidence-based knowledge exchange and knowledge transfer (Nutley et al, 2003; Bannister and Hardhill, 2015), and the eminent US evaluation theorist Carol Weiss also proposed a typology of evidence utilisation (Weiss, 1979). Drawing on this and other contributions (Weiss, 1980; Rossi et al, 2004; Nutley et al, 2007; Parsons and Thomas, 2015) implies that evaluators will find themselves in one of four decision-making contexts:

- *Evidence directed contexts*, where evaluation results are expected to be directly applied to a specific decision. For example, an intervention targeted with a required level of achievement and facing a funding decision to continue or drop the relevant activity, might rely solely on an economic or process evaluation of targeted outputs and any explanations for shortfall. However, this simple linear relationship between evidence and decision would be a rare situation facing evaluators today.
- *Political contexts* may see judgements about intervention effectiveness or effects driven by specific policy interests or ideology rather than evidence, but where evaluation may be harnessed tactically to justify decisions. This has been a common driver of policy-related evaluation in the past, but is less common with increasing public rights of access to publicly commissioned evidence (the Freedom of Information Act of 1967 and OPEN Government Act of 2007 in the US, and the UK Freedom of Information Act 2000).
- *Plural contexts*, where decision makers have sought evaluation evidence but expect their judgements to depend on information and influences drawn from a wider range of sources. Here the evaluation evidence will be harnessed alongside other influences such as stakeholder representation. This will be a common context for process, economic or impact evaluations.

- *Mandated evaluation contexts* arise where there is an accountability or other obligation from funders or policy makers for interventions to be evaluated at a fixed period or at close of funding. Here, decision makers have no choice but to take into account evaluation evidence but, as with plural contexts, they are likely to draw on evidence from other sources as well.

The scope for evaluators to be actively involved in optimising the use of evaluation findings is nil or negligible for evidence-directed or political contexts, but is stronger for plural or mandated contexts where decision makers will be juggling different influences. In these situations, evaluations may be providing the only systematic evidence on which decision makers can draw.

Type of evaluation

What form an evaluation itself takes may also influence the scope for an active role in helping decision makers unpick evidence and its implications. There is less scope where evaluation evidence aims to inform a very specific aspect required for decision-making, for example, where an RCT centres on a single outcome measurement (and where appropriate justified findings require little or no further interpretation by the evaluator).

Most evaluations, however, take place in more complicated circumstances reflected in more complex, multisource, multimode counterfactual designs, and taking into account a variety of influences or confounding variables. Here the evaluators may already have become active participants in the (subsequent) use of the evaluation by influencing expectations of what can be reasonably expected of the evidence and analysis. Post reporting, this interaction may be extended to help users better understand the evidence (and its strengths and weaknesses) on the balance of influences and the implications for decision-making.

User needs and specification

Evaluations that are based on coproduction or with extensive user–evaluator cooperation, perhaps through formative reporting, may have the opportunity to shape (or reshape, post-specification) user expectations of if and where active evaluator engagement is merited in better understanding evidence. However, the opportunities will often be constrained; users may not be open to evaluator engagement, or they may follow a rigid interpretation of the evaluation specification, anticipating that the evaluator's role ends with sign-off of a report. Even where there is a willingness to extend the evaluation role post-reporting, any supplementary inputs by the evaluator may need to be pro bono to avoid procurement rules or lengthy re-contracting. Not all evaluators will have the discretion, freedom or flexibility to do this.

Evaluation, and evaluators themselves, will be judged not just on providing deliverables to specification but by the quality and usefulness of what they provide. This brief review of user contexts shows that evaluators will have opportunities to take different roles and responsibilities according to the contexts in which the evaluation takes place. Being aware of these differences will help evaluators, acting always as the analyst not the decision maker, to anticipate those opportunities and adapt their 'reporting' role to optimise evaluation relevance and utility.

Deliverables and reporting outputs

The end product, or deliverable, of a summative evaluation is likely to be a final report, typically following one (or more) draft versions and perhaps supplemented with an executive summary. Formative evaluations usually require a little more, typically with one or more interim reports. For some evaluations this may be all that is expected, but commissioning bodies are more often asking evaluators to go further in producing, on time, a wider range of deliverables to support the exchange of evidence and findings. What is required will vary (substantially) from one evaluation to another, but may involve some combination of:

- summative factual reporting (in either comprehensive and/or summarised forms);
- outputs for effective management of the evaluation;
- developmental outputs including for staged factual reporting;
- themed outputs centred on specific factual content or implications;
- data-based outputs, perhaps for subsequent use and manipulation by users.

Figure 7.2 sets out common deliverables for each of these. This looks only at the most likely deliverables; users may also expect support for a range of supplementary deliverables and dissemination, and this is returned to later in this chapter. Main deliverables are usually written outputs or some form of other (usually oral) presentation, but social media and e-outputs are becoming important for supporting user dissemination.

This growing complexity of evaluation deliverables comes partly from rising demands for shorter, more digestible reports, with other materials (for example, narrative case studies) perhaps provided separately to avoid over-lengthening a final report. In longer or formative evaluations (typically lasting two years or more) users may also expect staged deliverables, not just interim reports but staged case studies, progress reports and perhaps presentations of early findings. Staged reporting expectations may need managing for realism and value. In a recent six-month impact evaluation of an outreach initiative by a large UK heritage organisation, an interim report was required just two weeks ahead of the draft final report – a time lag that would have allowed no time for any formative decision-making (the evaluators proposed a much less resource-extensive progress report instead).

A report structure may already be set out in the evaluation specification or at inception, but if not, evaluators are well advised to discuss and agree a structure well ahead of the report being produced.

Figure 7.2: Main deliverables from reporting

Nature of output	Purpose	Written	Oral	When delivered
Summative – comprehensive: - Final evaluation report - Technical report - Client/user or decision maker presentation - Dissemination, conference etc.	*Providing an end of evaluation presentation and explanation of findings and implications, together with critical review of strengths and weaknesses of evidence*	√ √ √ √	 √ √	End of project deliverables usually preceded by client sign-off from drafts
Summative – summary: - Executive summary - Summary report - Stakeholder (or other) brief	*Providing a synthesised version of findings and implications, usually for the purposes of wider briefing or communications*	√ √ √		Usually end of project
Evaluation management: - Routine or staged progress report - Annual review (longitudinal evaluation)	*Providing a periodic assessment of delivery of evaluation for contract management (by user) against delivery milestones and method plan (not usually reporting evidence)*	√ √	√ √	Key points of evaluation (may be linked to steering groups)

Figure 7.2: Main deliverables from reporting (continued)

Nature of output	Purpose	Written	Oral	When delivered
Developmental: - Staged or interim report - Deliberative workshop to assess early evidence - Staged presentation	*Providing a formative input to users for the purposes of interim review of evidence, informing mid-intervention improvements or shaping later stages of evaluation*	√ √	 √ √	Previously agreed points for interim decision-making
Themed: - Subsector, area or other 'mini' report - Presentation to subgroup (breakdown of evidence) - Practitioner or provider evaluation feedback	*Providing a formative or summative focus for specific segments of the user/stakeholder community likely to be affected by or interested in the evaluation*	√ √ √	 √ √	As agreed with client – may be formative but usually after completion of evaluation
Data: - Survey data, databases - Statistical source data or tabulations - Narrative case studies	*Providing source evidence (anonymised) to user to support in-house review*	√ √ √		End of project or (case studies only) on a staged basis

Requirements for other deliverables may be unclear and left vague some way into an evaluation (for example, end of project presentations). Multiple deliverables are an unavoidable fact of life for evaluations but increase the risk that evaluators may misunderstand what is required, and when. Each of these may need some clarification with users on exactly what is expected, its timing, who for and for what purpose.

Demonstrating reliability and validity

Beyond setting out findings and implications, evaluation reporting needs to demonstrate the quality of the design and the resulting evidence. This draws on what the evaluator will have already considered in their own assessment and testing of the quality of evidence, but it is a lot more than adding *p-values* drawn from analysis to tables in the report. Users should expect a full and frank review of quality; if this has slipped the attention of commissioners or the steering group, evaluators will need to be proactive in providing for this in reporting to support the evidence and conclusions.

Demonstrating quality usually focuses on two underpinning concepts of research design and use for both quantitative and qualitative (and mixed mode) designs:

- reliability of the methods or overall design
- validity of evidence or data.

Often, the terms may be used interchangeably, but to the evaluator they are quite separate; an evaluation measure may have strong validity but lack reliability, or have strong reliability but lack validity. Other measures of evidence quality could be brought in, such as accuracy, specificity and sensitivity (see Chapter 6) but too much detail can confuse users, and for most purposes reliability and validity assessments are adequate.

Just what do these statistical concepts mean for the evaluator? In essence, reliability is about the extent to which an evaluation design or specific method will give consistent results (if repeated in the same conditions) and describes the variance in data. Validity is about the strength of the evidence: how well-founded an evaluation indicator, measure, or piece of data is in representing what it is giving information on. John Ovretveit used a hypothetical example of 'data' on shooting target practice:

> An unreliable shooter is one whose shots are randomly spread across the target – and beyond. A reliable shooter will produce a concentration of shots in one area [of the target], but this may be way off centre. A valid shooter will produce a concentration of shots in the centre of the target. (Ovretveit, 1997, p 215)

How attention is given to reliability and variability in the reporting will vary with the nature of the evaluation, its design and user needs; each is worth a more detailed look.

Reliability

For more complex evaluations, and especially those using experimentation, large-scale surveys or data sets, statistical expertise may be needed for measuring reliability, perhaps through methods such as observer or *rater reliability* and *stability*. However, for all but the most complex evaluations, a more common sense approach is possible, and Figure 7.3 sets out what might be involved for five different aspects of reliability.

Analysing for reliability and demonstrating it appropriately in reporting is the conscience of an evaluation. It is a necessary but not sufficient step to laying the foundations for confidence and credibility, with demonstrating validity as an essential accompaniment.

Figure 7.3: Demonstrating reliability for an evaluation

Reliability	Quality review purpose	Common quality risks, ie. contrasts due to, for example...	Evaluation reporting needs
Subject reliability	Identifying any significant (in)consistencies due to the quality of data gathering in evaluation subjects	- Participant (beneficiary) motivations or fatigue - Participant recall or rationalisation - Attrition (longitudinal evaluation)	- Identification of known or likely evidence provision contrasts for subjects - Identification of (any) analysis controls
Observer reliability	Establishing any significant (in)consistencies that may be due to observer, rater or interviewer contrasts	- Inconsistent application by observer/interviewer - Different aptitude, levels of experience/skill of raters or interviewers - Differential interviewer briefing, engagement (or other bias)	- Identification of known or likely evidence recording contrasts by evidence gatherers - Estimation of reliability effects - Clarity on analysis control measures
Situational reliability	Acknowledging any significant (in)consistencies in the conditions under which evidence is gathered	- Different interviewing contexts - Different levels of support/engagement from providers - Historic (in evaluation) changes in evidence gathering context	- Identifying situational contrasts and any countermeasures to control for these

Figure 7.3: Demonstrating reliability for an evaluation (continued)

Reliability	Quality review purpose	Common quality risks, ie. contrasts due to, for example...	Evaluation reporting needs
Measurement reliability	Demonstrating consistency in use of the evidence gathering processes, indicators and evaluation instruments	- changed sampling or selection arrangements - changed participant motivation strategy (eg. incentives) - Inconsistent interpretation (bias) from poorly worded questions/ tools - Changed or adapted evaluation tools (longitudinal evaluations)	- Identification of measurement or instrumental contrasts (and reasons) - Estimation of evidence reliability effects
Analytical reliability	Demonstrating consistency in data preparation, processing and validity testing	- Inconsistent classification of evidence - Miscoding - Inconsistent use of validity or other statistical data tests	- Identification of data/analytical contrasts - Clarity on control measures

Validity

Demonstrating validity of evidence in reporting needs to take account of different influences and effects for:

- internal validity – which measures the trustworthiness of the data generated as a reflection of what had (or had not) happened in the specific evaluation context;
- external validity – which assesses the generalisability of findings and the confidence with which users can transfer the implications to other similar situations (for example, for rollout of a pilot nationally).

Figure 7.4 summarises what usually needs to be covered in reporting and some of the risks to be considered in sharing the validity of evidence with users.

Figure 7.4: Demonstrating validity for an evaluation

Validity	Quality review purpose	Common quality risks	Evaluation reporting needs
Internal validity	To demonstrate the extent to which the evaluation results (eg. achieved outputs and outcomes) and associations (cause-effect, enablers, constraints etc.) are a trustworthy reflection of what is being evaluated	- Situational change during the evaluation - Behavioural changes in provider/participant - Changes in measurement (or measurers) - Flawed randomisation - Inappropriate scale, sampling or selection - Flawed control or comparability	- Identification of measurement variability or constraints - Identifying 'internal' confounding influences on 'cause' and 'effect' in the reporting - Demonstrating testing for validity in the analysis (to critically review or strengthen results)
External validity	To demonstrate that the evaluation results for the (intervention) context can be confidently generalised to another similar context or situation	- Selection 'transferability' weaknesses for other contexts - Atypical comparative situation or context of evaluation evidence - Atypical evaluation measures or indicators for other situations - Scale biases (eg. likely changed effects between local/pilot transition to rollout)	- Clarity on internal measures/ assumptions in evaluation design - Identified limitations of evaluated evidence for anticipated (or likely) transfer situations - Clarity on likely transfer constraints (eg. prospective external changes)

Reporting validity will also need to set out what tests have been used to critically review or strengthen results. For example, with quantitative evidence it may help to 'cut' the data in different ways, perhaps by adapting classified data (for example, changing an age participation analysis from 'over 50' to 'over 55' and 'over 60') to see if this causes significant changes in the analysis. As with reliability, reporting of validity may end up being consigned to an annex of the final report or a separate technical report. Users may well be looking for a shorter and not overly technical main body of the report, but here it is possible to add health warnings and caveats where needed (perhaps as footnotes or endnotes), signposted to the fuller description in the annex or technical report.

Getting the report right

Whatever mixture of evaluation deliverables are involved, the evaluation report will remain centre stage. It is the key output of an evaluation, and all other deliverables will draw on it. Reduced to its essence it will need to present evidence and analysis geared to the evaluation objectives, and, taking account of reliability and validity, provide a concluding assessment of implications for decision-making. What the report says, and how the evidence is interpreted and used, will be the responsibility of the evaluator, but the reporting process will need some collaboration with the client organisation or user(s) if it is to be effective.

Why a collaboration, when it is the evaluator who knows the design and data (and its limitations) and has the analytical tools and the independence to set out robust conclusions and realisable proposals based on them? For the explanation we must return to the roots of evaluation – evidence to influence (better) decision-making and where the user best knows the circumstances underpinning the need for evidence, the sensitivities involved and the audience(s) intended. Users are also the gatekeepers to whatever institutional arrangements need to be negotiated to effectively harness the evaluation findings.

Some evaluators may prefer a completely hands-off arrangement, with very little and maybe no user collaboration, at least until after the draft report is produced. For them a user hands-off approach better demonstrates the total independence of the analysis. But independence does not require isolation from users, and it is not in the interests of maximising the use and value of an evaluation.

Users will also not favour isolation and evaluators will do well to recognise that to users the evaluation evidence may be threatening, and risks harm as well as help. In particular, users risk organisational disruption if findings are not wholly positive (and they rarely are). Users will also be conscious that providers risk losing roles and responsibilities (and contracts); beneficiaries may lose access to valued services; stakeholders risk seeing interventions in which they have a vested interest criticised as falling short of expectations. Of course, the reverse of all these is also a possibility, but users will be keen to ensure that it is not just the evaluation design that is fit for purpose; the presentation of the report will need to be as well. So some well-managed collaboration in how evidence and analysis is reported is desirable, and this may variously involve:

- advance agreement of an appropriate structure (and style) for the draft/final report;
- agreeing a precise reporting delivery schedule (draft, revised draft, final, etc);
- agreeing review arrangements, including query handling and responsiveness, receipt of comments, collation of comments and reconciliation of commentary etc;
- agreeing an editing protocol for evaluator feedback to the client or user on what has and has not been changed, and why.

Collaboration may also involve rehearsing the consequences of moving material to annexes or a technical report, as well as wider issues of dissemination. It may go further and an evaluator keen to see evidence harnessed may also be looking for a steer from the users on what areas of decision-making are expected, and when; who the key players are and what other influences are likely to be involved. Much of this will need to be negotiated; all of it will need anticipating, and some aspects may involve considerable lead times to securing agreement. None of this will take anything away from the evaluator's independence; nor should it be allowed to do so.

What should the report look like? This really is a case of 'horses for courses'; there is no universal template. Reports need to be customised and are likely to need to be shaped according to, in particular:

- what is being evaluated and the overall purpose of the evaluation;
- the external sensitivity or significance of the evaluation (which may require higher levels of proof and demonstration of validity);
- the evaluation design (both experimental and most economic evaluations need particularly careful rehearsal of evidence, assumptions, contingencies and testing);
- what evidence mix the evaluation involves (complex and multimode evaluations will have more to draw on, interrelate and present);
- The audience's ability to absorb the evidence and analysis (quantified analyses may need especially careful handling, presentation and explanation).

There are, nonetheless, some core content needs and requirements, as summarised in Figure 7.5.

As to the process of putting together an evaluation report (or other deliverables) and presenting findings, readers may bring already wide experience of doing this outside an evaluation context. Others can find a plethora of guidance from other sources. The aim here is to provide some insights into the reporting context for evaluators, and for making an effective start.

Figure 7.5: Structure and content for an evaluation report

Report section	Typical content	Some options
Preface	- Contents list and pagination - Acknowledgements - Preface or foreword	NB. A matter of personal style; but remember that this is an evidence reporting tool and not a book or research report
Summary	- Synthesised summary of full report – set out in 'read-across' subsections (to each main report section) - Content mainly by bullet points	- Substitute front-piece summary with opening key finding 'bullets' at start of each substantive chapter/section of main report
Introduction	- Brief statement of commissioning body (+ any other funding for evaluation) and with: - Background to what's being evaluated and the need for evaluation - Evaluation aims and objectives, with scope/any limitations to coverage - Report structure and signposting	- Consider adding any evaluation hypotheses (eg. for experimental evaluation) - Possible inclusion of/ signposting to intervention logic chart or rationale - Include short description of method (with longer annex)
Method and scope	- Standalone design/methodology description + reasons for choice - Evidence gathering focus (+ output and outcome measures/indicators) - Detailed description of data capture and analysis methods - Review of method effectiveness, including reliability and validity - Supporting/signposted content to any sensitivity analyses etc.	- For readability by non-technical audiences, put technical details of method application in footnotes or endnotes - For shorter main reports cross-reference to details in any evaluation framework/plan - Or, add short method statement to 'introduction' (fuller method description in annex)
Evidence analysis	- May be a single section in short reports/simple evaluations, or multiple in longer or more complex evaluations - Presentation balances coverage of key evidence with scope of evaluation + absorption potential of audience - Presentation of data to be agreed with the users (eg. graphical + detailed tabulations in one or more annexes)	- Where multiple sections divide either by evaluation objectives, themes or method strands (implementation vs control, survey, case studies etc.) - Use narrative 'quotes' (from interviews/case studies) to break up text and illustrate findings

Figure 7.5: Structure and content for an evaluation report (continued)

Report section	Typical content	Some options
Interpretation and conclusions	- Separated from evidence/data section(s) to differentiate reported 'fact' from evaluator 'interpretation' - Provides crosscutting (triangulated) analysis across sections/evidence - Conclusions and interpretations (judgements) set against individual evaluation objectives or criteria	- For shorter main reports add 'overview' sections (bullets?) at end of each main-body section
Proposals or recommendations	- Standalone review of implications for decision-making - Signpost each individual proposal to evidence section/conclusion(s) - Balance strength of evidence with practicality of proposals - Careful use of language – make proposals 'SMART' (see Chapter 2)	- For short reports/less complex evaluations include 'recommendations' as a concluding subsection under 'analysis and conclusions' - Suggestions for further evidence gathering/research can be added – where directly relevant to proposed actions
Annexes	- Multiple annexes presented in sequence with reference in main body - Provide essential supporting material/ data/evidence to support main-body presentation/analysis - Might include formal evaluation brief, review of methodology, evidence validity testing results, supporting data/key tabulations and p-tests), or lists of engaged participants (if not confidential)	- Possible addition of copies of evaluation instruments - For brevity of main report, full case studies may be annexes - Where relevant (external credibility), ethics clearances may be added here - Where there are multiple/ long annexes consider replacing some/all with a separate technical report

Going beyond reporting

This chapter started with the idea that reporting on an evaluation is a necessary but (often) insufficient end point for supporting evidence-based decision-making. A 100 or 200 page (or larger) report may contain all that users should need to understand the evidence, its validity and implications, and may even be read in full by a handful of people, but standing on its own it may not be doing enough to inform time-pressed decision-makers juggling other pressures. How and how far should evaluators be prepared to go beyond reporting? In some evaluation situations, the scope may be limited, especially where the evaluation:

- has a simple and straightforward (easily comprehensible) design, or is small-scale (small-n);
- is centred on an intervention and policy context that are not sensitive;
- produces findings that are mainly positive for all stakeholders.

Here, users may need little more than some traditional dissemination support from evaluators, perhaps a summary report, a presentation to decision-makers and/or stakeholders, and perhaps input into a press release. Where the users have an open approach to, or specific interest in, sharing evidence and knowledge exchange, evaluators may also have the chance for some wider dissemination of their efforts through journal or conference papers.

Yet evaluations are often not simple and straightforward; they may have complex and multifaceted designs, and take place in sensitive or challenging policy circumstances. They could be surrounded by vested interests, where stakeholders have different and perhaps entrenched views on 'what works' for an intervention, and which the evaluation evidence may challenge. Here, stronger action than dissemination is needed both to explain complex findings and to build wider confidence and credibility in the evidence and its implications.

In these situations, going beyond reporting often needs evaluators to support a more diverse approach, moving away from a traditional approach to dissemination to one based on evidence sharing (and review) through 'communication'. This is likely to be based on:

a mutual exchange of knowledge between researchers and practitioners at different stages throughout the research (evaluation) process (Nutley et al, 2007, p 27)

This will go beyond a report, summary and press release, and will involve a mix of a wider range of methods of knowledge transfer and exchange. Figure 7.6 sets out some of the likely options. This is not an exhaustive list but it does show that, unlike dissemination, this is not wholly an end-of-evaluation activity, with evaluators possibly progressively engaging with users to build understanding of emerging findings.

A communications-led approach has two other great advantages. The first is that it better accommodates the changing way in which funders, decision makers, operating managers, practitioners and others acquire and search for knowledge. Fast spread and absorption of information through online mechanisms and social media are facts of life. Embracing the potential of online communication, in its multiplicity of possibilities, is consequently an important part of widening the exchange (and use) of evaluation messages. This is especially important post reporting and where implications (for example, better practice evidence) needs to get to a wider and perhaps hard-to-reach community (for example, provider managers or professionals).

Figure 7.6: Some pre and post reporting evaluation communication options

Medium	Audience reached	Method(s)
Written press releases and briefings	- All - Fragmented non-policy audiences - Practitioners	- Open and segmented press releases - Pre-release briefings (+ access to lead evaluator)
Policy/ practice briefs	- Cascade briefing (users/ stakeholders) - Wider policy, practice or professional audiences - Consultants	- Tailor briefs to specific or priority user audiences - Keep facts punchy; emphasise 'implications' and proposals
Newsletters/e-bulletins	- Policy advisors, consultants and practitioners in niche/ specialist groups - Priority audiences or wider coverage	- Harness stakeholder contacts to access specific newsletters etc.
Presentations (oral)	- All (where there is open access to launch event, roadshows, workshops etc.) - Evaluation advisory/steering group (pre-reporting) - Internal policy team, advisors, account managers etc. (post-report – pre-launch) - Professional body, provider or practice/sector group leaders	- Internal (user) briefings - Launch conference, post-launch (rollout) stakeholder workshops - Rollout events (with embedded evaluation element) - Representative workshops (sector/professional) [representative workshops group?] - Priority group seminars - Other segmented presentations etc.
User/ stakeholder websites	- In-house rollout for users/ core stakeholders - Provider managers, practitioners and consultants	- Customise existing comms material for user/stakeholder segments (eg. press release or policy briefs)

Figure 7.6: Some pre and post reporting evaluation communication options (continued)

Medium	Audience reached	Method(s)
e-fora	- All - Widening access outside 'usual culprits' - Hard-to-identify users/ practitioners	- LinkedIn fora - Special interest e-fora - Online discussion groups and online Q&A
Blogs, podcasts	- All - Non-engaged practitioners	- Can be used to maintain communications momentum
Twitter and misc. social media	- All - Wider access to provider managers/practitioners - Hard-to-identify users/ practitioners	- Low investment, wide distribution but highly condensed 'single messages'
Practice toolkits, guidelines	- Practice managers - Practitioners	- Specialist evidence-based guidance for wider users (eg. better practice)

The second advantage is that stronger communications can help decision makers to prepare for and accommodate negative as well as positive findings. While it is overly simplistic to polarise the results of an evaluation into 'positive' and 'negative', effectively communicating adverse outcomes is an important issue for evaluators keen to maximise the use of findings. This may also preoccupy users long before an evaluation reports. Experience shows that negative findings need to be understood by the stakeholders concerned, and a transparent, two-way, active and constructive approach to communicating these underpins how stakeholders can start to relate more positively to them.

Not all evaluators will feel comfortable with going beyond reporting through more active communications. This may even have implications for the skills of the evaluation team. But active communication helps evaluators maximise the potential for findings being used. This is about much more than knowledge exchange. It helps evaluations build the necessary confidence and credibility in all findings, which is necessary for decision-making.

8

EMERGING CHALLENGES FOR EVALUATION AND EVALUATORS

- Moving beyond ad hoc evaluation by integrating development and policy design
- Balancing rising user expectations with diminishing resources
- Shortening decision-making timeframes and possibilities for real-time analysis
- Building confidence and credibility through proactive engagement in evaluation
- Tackling relativism and proportionality imaginatively and constructively
- Next steps for evaluators, professional networking and guidance

Introduction

The previous chapters show how evaluators now have a lot of options and consequently choices to make, to compile, compose and conduct an evaluation that can bring robust and credible evidence into decision-making. These options have greatly expanded in the last two decades especially, and they will no doubt develop further in the next 10 to 20 years. It is beyond this author to predict how scholars and practitioners will add to these opportunities, but it is possible to take a forward look at some of the issues they will be responding to. The space and time available here can only scratch the surface of the challenging and often exciting possibilities that readers may face. What is clear is that evaluators who are able to think robustly, responsively and creatively will be in demand.

Integrating development and evaluation design

If it were possible to condense good design of evaluation into a handful of rules, perhaps the first would be 'timing is everything'. The UK's Magenta Book, the evaluation handbook for those in government (and outside) puts it this way:

> the design and implementation of a policy affects how reliably it can be evaluated, and even quite minor adjustments to the way a policy is implemented can make the difference between being able to produce a reliable evaluation … and not being able to produce any meaningful evidence. (HM Treasury, 2011, p 25)

This is a sound caution and points to the need for good evaluation to be designed alongside an intervention and not as an afterthought. However, even within government, in the UK and outside, other considerations often come ahead of taking this into account. Outside central government it is all too rarely observed. The result is that too often evaluators find themselves coming late to the party; the intervention is planned and may have been running for months (or years) before the evaluators are called in. Coming in late often means shorter timescales, compromised designs and diminished method options and opportunities. In this state of play robust experimental designs (for impact evaluation) are likely to be impossible. Early process or start-up evidence on, for example, costs and use of resources may be lost or compromised; partners and players (managers, practitioners and beneficiaries) may have moved on.

This is not an emerging challenge for evaluators; it is a real and present one. The challenge is changing this state of play, by better integrating evaluation in policy or programme development with the anticipation of evaluation needs running in parallel with the design of an intervention. Where an organisation is large enough to have in-house evaluation expertise this is an internal issue for organisational priorities and planning. In this situation, there will also be an issue for championing the value to decision-making of acting early enough to avoid compromising on evaluation designs. Such champions might also encourage policy makers to value accumulation of evaluation evidence with policies best informed not on the back of evidence from one evaluation of a single evaluation but progressive accumulation of evidence over different circumstances and time.

Elsewhere, and in most organisations commissioning and using evaluations, the challenge of integrating development with evaluation design is similar but often lacks leadership or specialist knowledge. For some, the way forward may be to look to a new role of external advisor to work with policy and programme developers in-house to integrate and support earlier evaluation decision-making more effectively. This may not fit all organisations; some will be resistant to changing existing relationships and influences. But where organisations are open to change, improved support for evaluation design at an early stage could bring benefits in more sophisticated, more timely and probably more cost-effective, designs and support to decision makers.

Where should these 'new' advisors come from? The best candidates will most probably be found within the existing evaluator community. Not all will be suited or ready for such a role and most may prefer to stay inside their comfort zone (they could hardly advise on and also conduct the evaluations they were helping to shape). Others will be willing and able, and for some organisations regularly commissioning and using external evaluators, tapping this capability will perhaps be the next big step they need to consider in building and sustaining better evaluation-based decision-making.

Rising expectations, diminishing resources

As a young policy researcher, 30 years ago, the author was asked to put together a proposal and budget for an (ex ante) evaluation of the labour market impacts of an international airport development. There was no brief, no set budget, no set timeframe and certainly no invitation to tender. As a starting point for an evaluation this situation would be incomprehensible now. Not only would it be in breach of a raft of procurement rules, rising public agency cost and timing pressures mean that budget and timeframe would be probably be squeezed and almost certainly fixed. Future evaluators are highly unlikely to see these new realities change, and the pressures on costs and timeframes are here to stay, for three reasons:

- **Downward pressures on (evaluation) costs within funded programmes:** Many and probably most evaluations in social and policy contexts are funded directly or indirectly through public or charitable funding, where there is acute pressure on budgets, demands for value for money, limits on expenditure and increased accountability. Evaluation funds may be drawn from 'top-slicing' overall programme budgets, with the result that a bigger or more costly evaluation activity will see the programme being able to do or deliver less to fewer beneficiaries. Although sensible for the quality of decision-making, the case for 'more evaluation, less delivery' has always been difficult to make, especially if programme costs themselves are being squeezed by austerity or other expenditure cuts.
- **Departmental budgetary constraints on 'research and consulting':** If not funded through programme funds, evaluation may draw on separately allocated departmental budgets for 'research', 'research and consultancy' or 'monitoring and research'. Across the developed economies, public sector organisations have often looked to these 'overheads' budgets first to take the brunt of 'austerity' or efficiency cuts to public funding. Accompanying this, public bodies may tighten the rules

on budgetary discretion for all but the most senior managers, with the result that more and more evaluation budgets are being set below those (low) spending authority levels for officials or managers. Few have the time, enthusiasm or confidence for making a special case for an evaluation budget to exceed those authorities.

• **Shortening decision-making cycles:** Independent of these expenditure constraints, the timeframes for conducting evaluations have been driven down by commissioners and users who are keen to get evidence (more) speedily. More compressed timescales ratchet up intensity but often ask no less of the evaluator in quality expectations, evidence gathering and deliverables. In the public sector, political cycles are largely unchanged (fixed term governments; quadrennial or quinquennial election of regional, state or local governments) but policy cycles have generally intensified. Policies and interventions are expected to be able to 'wash their face' and show viability or value in shorter timeframes, and evaluations necessarily follow these shorter decision-making cycles.

It is difficult to escape the likelihood that evaluators will continue to be caught in the squeeze between rising expectations and often ambitious demands for evidence collection and reporting, and doing so with a limited budget and compressed timeframes. How can this challenge be addressed? For traditional evaluators, this will seem an unholy combination, where the downward pressures on costs and timeframes need to be resisted. On occasion, questioning budgets or delivery expectations might lead to commissioners rethinking, but experience suggests this is uncommon and the hands of commissioners themselves are often tied by previously set budgetary constraints and rules.

More embedded approaches to evaluation (see below) may help in some situations, but will require systems investments which may be difficult to achieve when there are other demands on investment. Designs using more cost-effective methods (e-surveys, online data collection and processing), smaller samples or leaner reporting, for example, may also help, but the further scope for this may already be limited and is likely to be impossible for experimental evaluations, and may be ill-advised elsewhere. Economies in the scale or depth of evidence reporting, which are a heavy demand on evaluators' resources, may also help but will inevitably lead to less analytical flexibility, and reduced certainty and confidence.

Perhaps the most constructive way of better balancing rising expectations with diminishing resources is through better integration of policy or programme development with evaluation design (as above). However, until evaluation becomes more widely valued as an essential management and probity tool, within many commissioning bodies, this will remain countercultural for many. At best it will take time to realise. Until then, this expectations–resource squeeze is not going away, and it will be a continuing headache for evaluators, placing greater demands on their skills and creativity in mixing methodologies and managing expectations.

Timeframes and real-time analysis

Alongside shortening timeframes for evaluations, sits a thirst for intelligence (and perhaps reassurance) about how well new initiatives and interventions are working against expectations. The time has long gone when policy makers and programme funders would put effort into comprehensive piloting and aligning rollout of programmes and then sit back and wait for sensible evaluation findings to help them judge what was working and how it might be improved. Evaluation is not yet expected to provide for 'real-time' assessment, but one of the emerging challenges may be for more regularised and embedded approaches to evidence gathering to support the growing intensity needed for evidence turnaround.

This book has taken for granted the expectation that effective evaluation is customised evaluation, geared to meet specific decision-making needs for particular intervention circumstances and contexts. Customisation is a sound principle. It is a foundation for the standalone approach, which bases evaluation practice on individual, tailored evaluations, usually specific and with a defined start and finish. While this is likely to continue to be the focus for most future evaluation activity, there may be scope to tap developments in more cost-effective data gathering, 'big data' accumulation and real-time processing, to provide for alternative and embedded approaches where this is practical.

An embedded evaluation shares some common ground with monitoring, where core data needs are fixed firmly and deeply in the practice and delivery of an evaluation. This will usually be data–based: centred on inputs and outputs, often set against delivery expectations or targets, and/or to meet specific management information needs. Such embedded evidence is readily tapped by most process evaluations – although they will usually go further to capture data from a wider range of sources. However, the concept can be widened to support evaluation, not just internal monitoring, and also extended to support elements of impact assessment. This remains unusual, but one example is the integrated model for impact evaluation used by the UK's Waste and Resources Action Programme, which is shown in Example 12 below.

Example 12: WRAP's approach to embedded (integrated) impact evaluation

The Waste and Resources Action Programme (WRAP) in the UK coordinates a wide range of waste avoidance, recycling and reuse initiatives across industry and domestically, and since 2007 has been using an (evolving) embedded approach to impact evaluation to assess the effectiveness of its diverse (mainly) publicly funded programmes. Evaluation is (mainly) through an integrated, data-led and theory-based cross-programme model, supplemented with occasional bespoke programme evaluations. WRAP has seven principles underpinning this model: theory-based, evidence-based, nation-specific, attribution-centred, annualised and lifetime reporting, avoiding double-counting, and reporting uncertainty levels.

The approach has developed over the last seven years and is based on identifying (and collecting data for) core outputs and outcomes across all non-consumer WRAP programmes (earlier testing had suggested the integrated model was not suitable for more volatile consumer-facing campaigns). Data is captured and processed through a bespoke database, with evidence coming from key stakeholder monitoring, an annualised programme of semi-structured beneficiary interviews, ad hoc (occasional) independent evaluations, and external benchmarks. The model includes some annual flexibility to meet specific programme or activity requirements or ad hoc themes, and the annualised interviews provide for some evidence of indirect (or unintended) consequences. Attribution evidence (counterfactual) is drawn from self-reported beneficiary assessments.

Earlier versions of the model (and reporting from it) successfully included process evidence, but funders' demands have seen an increasing focus on impact measurement. The model combines year-on-year consistency for common indicators with flexibility to add (some) differentiated information needs through the (annually adjusted) beneficiary interviews. Reporting provides gross and net impact estimates for individual programmes and home country breakdowns, based on both current assessments of outcomes, together with extrapolations (from the time series now available) five to six years ahead, to assess trajectories and likely longer-term effects.

Embedded evaluation is unlikely to deliver the range of evidence or insights of a well-designed, well-resourced standalone evaluation. It will not fit all circumstances, but it will have potential where an organisation has multiple programmes with similar high-level goals that need regular evaluation (tracking) across similar sets of beneficiary groups and stakeholders. A lot more evidence is going to be needed to see if and where embedding will be useful, although it is clear that such techniques are not consistent with experimental approaches, the rigour needed for economic evaluation or with interventions likely to secure small net impacts. However, they may be used to support a mixed mode approach to assessing progress and achievements over time and to understanding effectiveness. The embedded approach could also be combined with more highly targeted standalone evaluation and to support greater cost-efficiencies in standalone evaluation – as it has for WRAP.

Confidence, credibility and engagement in evaluation

One traditional view of evaluation has the evaluators keeping their distance from users, observing strict rules of (dis)engagement with providers and stakeholders, and applying structured protocols for any interaction with beneficiaries. For a few, notably in academia, and for some in government favouring what has been called *neutral assessment* (Treasury Board of Canada Secretariat, 2012), this was to ensure proof of total independence of the evaluation and nil risk of evidence distortion. Of course, even if this were an ideal, it may rarely have been achieved in practice, but the ideas continue to influence how engagement and independence in evaluations are perceived.

Today's (and tomorrow's) demands on evaluators are pressing in the opposite direction from separation, and the quality of engagement and the working relationships developed with stakeholders are increasingly central to the success of evaluation. This is an important and valuable shift in emphasis for evaluators. Engagement offers many advantages to the evaluators in better understanding the programme field and underpinning mechanisms of change in what is being evaluated, and using this to provide for a more informed analysis of determinants and causation. It also offers potential for optimising the likely use of that interpretation (and findings) at its conclusion.

Being able to respond effectively to the potential for constructive engagement calls for some fresh thinking on how engagement needs to be managed without compromising the necessary separation of analysis and interpretation. For some this will present challenges in recalibrating just what is meant (and needed) in relation to evaluators' independence, as well as developing additional skill sets (for example, confidence in negotiation and expectations management) to be able to:

- balance users 'wants' with the practical possibilities for informing necessary decision making – users' actual achievable 'needs' through expectations management;
- maximise the potential for use of findings in decision-making through more creative and progressive communications;

- raise confidence and credibility in findings, and doing so across the whole evaluation process (not just in reporting).

Chapter 3 has already covered the first of these, and Chapter 7 looked at the issues of smarter communications approaches to maximise evaluation use and utility; neither needs adding to further here. Engagement to raise confidence and credibility merits a little more attention.

Confidence and credibility have tended to be regarded as technical issues for proving the quality of evidence, reliability and validity. As the preceding chapter shows, these remain important issues but overreliance on these technical foundations risks evaluators neglecting other underpinnings. It may never have been enough for evaluators to technically 'prove' that findings can be treated with confidence, but in the social and policy world it is set to be increasingly side-lined by scepticism, distrust (among some) of experts (evaluators), their methods and data, as well as other 'political' considerations. Scepticism will be added to where stakeholders' subjective or self-interested viewpoints are countered or contradicted by evaluation evidence. In short, evaluators need to engage with users and stakeholders early and progressively, and in ways that help prepare the ground for evidence and its implications to be accepted, and acted upon.

The previous chapter suggested that some in evaluation will see this as 'not my job'. However, evaluators who stand back may expose their findings to criticism from those who may not like some of the findings, or simply do not understand them. If those voices are influential, even well-founded findings may be unfairly tarnished and discounted in decision-making. Without engagement by evaluators, the risks intensify that rational evidence will lose out to what may be vested interests and even prejudice.

So, how could evaluators better engage to minimise these risks? Experience suggests this needs to be proactive, planned and start early if it is to help in building confidence and credibility, ideally before designs are put in place. Effective engagement will recognise that the evaluation process from start to finish will directly influence user expectations, and that it is positively influenced by:

- developing a clear, shared, well-communicated sense of purpose for the evaluation;
- establishing a relevant, decision-centred scope and focus for the evaluation, with methods understood (at least in outline) by users and key stakeholders;
- open and effective planning to demonstrate robustness in design and implementation, and where possible a commitment to co-creation;
- effective mapping and (proactive) engagement of primary *and* secondary users;
- previewed findings to share early issues and emerging implications;
- trusted analysis and analyst(s) – demonstrating independence and impartiality;
- user-orientated representation of evidence and its limitations;
- effective and usually multi-deliverable communication of findings (the right media for the right audiences).

Evaluators will not have a free hand in all of this, and their engagement usually needs to be negotiated with clients and users who will have a more direct (although not always constructive) interest in issues of engagement. Where tackling engagement is likely to work well, it is most likely to involve appropriately wide stakeholder interests (within the scope of the evaluation) and will directly involve doubters (and doubts) as well as natural supporters of the evaluation and the evidence it will be producing.

Relativism and proportionality

Nobody that I am aware of knows how to solve the thorny dilemma of rising expectations of evaluation, set against diminishing resources to underpin them. Whatever path individual evaluators take, the first step is to accept that these are changes that are here to stay and for which idealistic, revisionist or simplistic solutions offer little or nothing for the longer term.

Perhaps addressing these challenges means we are moving towards some new paradigm, as evaluation practices become more mainstream in the development of social policy and programmes. This book started with the goal of working across different theoretical approaches to evaluation and it will not conclude with proposing some new all-embracing theory, even if one were apparent. Instead it would seem best to conclude that evaluation ideas and practices evolve, and the challenges of more integrated, leaner, embedded or engaged approaches will provide further impetus for it to do so.

Practice will not change of itself. It is for evaluators to offer solutions that balance needs, resources and circumstances. Being willing and able to question commissioners' assumptions and expectations will be a good starting point. As Carol Weiss pointed out in a prospective view of evaluation challenges some years ago:

> evaluators do not have to be passive in accepting whatever conditions the sponsor sets. They can argue back, explain that the time is too short, the requisite data are unavailable, appropriate comparisons are missing, the money is insufficient for the size of the task, or whatever the problems may be. (Weiss, 1998b, p 3)

However, it seems such negotiation needs to be framed in a spirit of *relativism*. This would start with the assumption that there is no absolute truth to be sought from an ideal evaluation approach to a particular situation, and that truth is always relative to the limited nature of the intervention and policy or other framework in which it is set. It will also be relative to the timing, intervention situation, and decision-making framework with which the evaluation is engaged – all things which 'design' cannot change. This truth will also be limited by whatever proportional approach to evaluation design is chosen.

In terms of evidence paradigms, am I therefore proposing all evaluation design needs to be interpretivist? Will future evaluations largely abandon the positivist approaches (see Chapter 2) that underpin experimental evaluation designs? No, neither paradigm wholly fits the constrained and applied world that new evaluators will occupy, and in all likelihood, nor have they ever done so. I am suggesting that the intensifying demands and practical pressures on evaluators call for all designs to be framed as relativist. Looked at in this way, all evaluation design – experimental or not – will involve a structured approach to compromise, with evaluators responsible for framing the best design (and expectations aligned with this) but also to set out valid findings within those limitations, openly sharing the limitations and relative nature of the work.

If relativism is to be a touchstone for addressing challenges, then design solutions (and evaluation procurement and management) will commonly need to be based on a stronger and more structured approach to proportionality. There is surprisingly little advice on proportionality in evaluation practice (although hopefully Chapter 3 helps), but it hinges on needs-driven choices, combining smarter use of (often) mixed modes, underpinned by early and open dialogue between users and evaluators on options and analytical consequences. Some might say that principles of good evaluation design have always been proportionate; true or not, relativism and proportionality are set to be cornerstones of maturing evaluation practices.

Next steps

The book is part of a 'shorts' series, aimed at unlocking some of the confusions and apparent contradictions that readers will come across in taking their early steps with evaluation. There is much, much more it could have covered. Hopefully, the selection of what is likely to be most useful helps to demystify evaluation for those new to it, or with limited experience, and those commissioning and using evaluations perhaps for the first time. The references built into the chapters draw on a lot of practical wisdom and provide an opportunity for readers to dig deeper, and I do encourage readers to do so.

Beyond this, there is much practical guidance that can and should be taken into account, and valuable next steps for new evaluators might include:

- Harnessing the solid guidance available in some of the excellent practical guides and toolkits aimed especially at programme evaluators – like the UK's *Magenta Book*: www. gov.uk/government/uploads/system/uploads/attachment_data/ file/220542/magenta_book_combined.pdf. This is produced by the UK's Treasury department (HM Treasury) for the benefit of civil servants and others in non-executive government agencies, but has much wider application, with separate sections for those using evaluation or policy staff and designers. The US Government's Accountability Office also produces a similar practitioner guide on *Designing Evaluations* (2012), which can be accessed as a pdf: http://www.gao.gov/assets/590/588146.pdf
- In devolved and federal government there may be individual states producing their own governmental guidance, some of which can be quite extensive, for example, the Australian New South Wales Government guidance: www.dpc.nsw.gov. au/__data/assets/pdf_file/0009/155844/NSW_Government_ Program_Evaluation_Guidelines.pdf
- Joining and taking advantage of one of the professional bodies, in particular, the American Evaluation Association (www.eval.org), the European Evaluation Society (www.europeanevaluation. org) or the UK Evaluation Society (www.evaluation.org.uk). All are concerned with providing a cross-disciplinary focus for practitioners at all levels of experience to improve the knowledge of theory, practice and use of evaluation. National evaluation associations elsewhere – for example, the Australasian Evaluation Society (www.aes.asn.au) – also produce their own guidance and support communities of interest responsive to national circumstances.
- Checking any more localised or specific guidance and requirements, either for specific government departments and

agencies directly sponsoring or with a close interest in what is being evaluated, or individual funding bodies, trusts and foundations which may have their own evaluation guidance and standards. While such guidance is likely to be less extensive than the sources cited above, these organisations may have specific requirements for, for example, impact indicators, design or ethical requirements, or reporting needs, which need to be understood (and complied with).

Those evaluators working in the domain of foreign or international development will have other guidance to explore, taking account of the very specific circumstances and needs of programme evaluation in international aid contexts. Here, although there are other guides, the Organisation for Economic Co-operation and Development (OECD) has produced, through its Development Assistance Committee (DAC), the so-called DAC *Quality Standards for Development Evaluation*: www. oecd.org/development/evaluation/qualitystandards.pdf

It will come as no surprise that the perhaps eclectic approach of this book avoids pointing to any one of these sources; all have a role to play in helping further inform and steer evaluators' choices. Perhaps the best final word is to say that, as with choices of methods, the guiding rule for what further guidance to follow is 'horses for courses'. The art of critically informed judgement underpins much in successful evaluation; and it should also drive readers' own next steps to build their knowledge and stretch their methodological and analytical horizons, to the benefit of future evidence-based decision-making.

References

American Evaluation Association (2004) *General principles for evaluators*, Washington, DC: AEA.

Attwood, H. (1997) 'An overview of issues around the use of participatory approaches by post-graduate students', in Institute for Development Studies, *Participatory research, IDS PRA topic pack*, Brighton: IDS, University of Sussex.

Bannister, J. and Hardhill, I. (2015) 'Knowledge mobilisation and the social sciences: dancing with new partners in an age of austerity', in J. Bannister and I. Hardhill (eds) *Knowledge mobilisation and the social sciences: Research, impact and engagement*, Oxford: Taylor & Francis, pp 71–79.

Bryman, A. (2012) *Social research methods* (4th edn), Oxford: Oxford University Press.

Byrne, D. (2009) 'Case-based methods: why we need them; what they are; how to do them?' in D. Byrne and C.C. Ragin (eds) *The SAGE handbook of case-based methods*, London: Sage, pp 1–10.

Campbell, D. and Fiske, D. (1959) 'Convergent and discriminant validation by the multi trait-multimethod matrix', *Psychological Bulletin*, 56(2): 81–105.

Campbell, D. and Stanley, J. (1966) *Experimental and quasi-experimental designs for research*, Chicago, IL: Rand-McNally.

Canadian Evaluation Society (2015) What is Evaluation? CES. October 2015. Renfrew (Ontario), http://evaluationcanada.ca/sites/default/files/ces_def_of_evaluation_201510.pdf

Charlesworth, A. (2014) *Data protection and research data*, Cheltenham: Joint Information Services Committee, https://www.jisc.ac.uk/full-guide/data-protection-and-research-data

Chelimsky, E. and Shadish, W.R. (eds) (1997) *Evaluation in the 21st century: A handbook*, Thousand Oaks, CA: Sage.

Chen, H.T. (1990) *Theory-driven evaluation*, Newbury Park, CA: Sage.

Clarke, A. (1999) *Evaluation research*, London: Sage

Cook, T. and Campbell, D. (1979) *Quasi-experimental design and analysis issues for field settings*, Boston, MA: Houghton Mifflin Company.

Cousins, B. and Leithwood, K. (1986) 'Current empirical research on evaluation utilisation', *Review of Educational Research*, 56(3): 331–64.

Creswell, J. (1994) *Research design: Qualitative and quantitative approaches*. Thousand Oaks, CA: SAGE.

Creswell, J. (2003) *Research design: Qualitative, quantitative, and mixed method approaches* (2nd edn), Thousand Oaks, CA: SAGE.

Denzin, N.K. (1970) *The Research Act: A theoretical introduction to sociological methods*, New York: McGraw Hill.

Denzin, N.K. and Lincoln, Y.S. (2000) *Handbook of qualitative research* (2nd edn), Thousand Oaks, CA: Sage.

Dolan, P. and Peasgood, T. (2007) 'Estimating the economic and social costs of the fear of crime', *The British Journal of Criminology*, 47: 121–32.

Drummond, M., Sculpher, M., Torrance, G., O'Brien, B. and Stoddart, G. (2005) *Methods for the economic evaluation of health care programmes* (3rd edn), Oxford: Oxford University Press.

Fox, C., Grimm, R. and Rute, C. (2016) *An introduction to evaluation*, London: Sage.

Gillespie, G. (1991) *Manufacturing knowledge: A history of the Hawthorne experiments*, Cambridge: Cambridge University Press.

Government Social Research Unit (2007) *Why do social experiments: Experiments and quasi-experiments for evaluating government policies and programmes*, Government Social Research Unit Background Paper No. 7, London: Cabinet Office.

Guba, E.G. and Lincoln, Y.S. (1989) *Fourth generation evaluation*. Newbury Park, CA: Sage.

Hall, I. and Hall, D. (2004) *Evaluation and social research: Introducing small-scale practice*, Basingstoke: Palgrave Macmillan.

Harris, E., Noble, J. and Hodgson, L. (2012) *Creating your theory of change: NPC's practical guide*, NPC: London.

Haynes, L., Service, O., Goldacre, B. and Torgerson, D. (2012) *Test, Learn, Adapt: Developing public policy with randomised controlled trials*, London: Cabinet Office.

Hill, M. and Hupe, P. (2014) *Implementing public policy*, London: Sage.

HM Treasury (2011) *The magenta book: Guidance for evaluation*, London: HM Treasury, www.gov.uk/government/uploads/system/uploads/attachment_data/file/220542/magenta_book_combined.pdf

HM Treasury (2013) *The green book: Appraisal and evaluation in central government*, London: TSO, www.gov.uk/government/uploads/system/uploads/attachment_data/file/220541/green_book_complete.pdf

HMSO (1999) *Modernising government*, London: HMSO.

ISO (2015) *Information Security Management. International Organisation for Standards*, Geneva, www.iso.org/iso/iso27001

Lewin, K. (1946) 'Action research and minority problems', *Journal of Social Issues*, 2(4): 34–46.

Kara, H. (2016) *Creative research methods in evaluation: A practical guide*, Bristol: Policy Press.

Kemmis, S. and McTaggart, R. (2005) 'Communicative action and the public sphere', in N.K. Denzin and Y.S. Lincoln (eds) *The Sage handbook of qualitative research*, London: Sage, 559–603.

Kubisch, A. (1997) *Voices from the field: Learning from the early work of comprehensive community initiatives*, Washington, DC: Aspen Institute.

MacDonald, C. (2012) 'Understanding participatory action research: a qualitative research methodology option', *Canadian Journal of Action Research*, 13(2): 34–50.

Marchal, B., Belle, S., Olmen, J., Hoeree, T. and Kegels, G. (2012) 'Is realist evaluation keeping its promise? A review of published empirical studies in the field of health systems research', *Evaluation*, 18(2): 119–212.

Market Research Society and Social Research Association (2013) *Data Protection Act 1998: Guidance for social researchers*, London: MRS/SRA, http://the-sra.org.uk/wp-content/uploads/MRS-SRA-DP-Guidelines-updated-April-2013.pdf

Marshall, J. (2001) 'Self-reflective inquiry practices', in P. Reason and H. Bradbury (eds) *Handbook of action research: Participative Inquiry and Practice,* London: Sage, pp 433–9.

Mason, J. (2002) Qualitative researching, (2nd ed), London: Sage.

Mayne, J. (2001) 'Addressing attribution through contribution analysis: using performance measures sensibly', *Canadian Journal of Programme Evaluation*, 16: 1–24. Earlier version available at www.oagbvg.gc.ca/domino/other.nsf/html/99dp1_e.html/$file/99dp1_e.pdf

Mayne, J. and Rist, R.C. (2006) 'Studies are not enough: the necessary transformation of evaluation', *Canadian Journal of Programme Evaluation*, 21: 93–120.

Mertens, D.M and Wilson, A.T. (2012) *Program evaluation theory and practice: A comprehensive guide*, New York: Guildford Press.

Murphy, S. Moore, G.F., Tapper, K., Lynch, R. Clarke, R., Raisanen, L. Desousa, C. and Moore, L. (2007) 'Free healthy breakfasts in primary schools: a cluster randomised controlled trial of a policy intervention in Wales', *Public Health Nutrition*, 14(2): 219–26.

New Brunswick Declaration (2013) *New Brunswick Declaration on Research Ethics, Integrity and Governance,* Ethics Rupture Summit Declaration, New Brunswick, Canada, January 2013.

Nicholls, J., Lawlor, E., Neitzert, E. and Goodspeed, T. (2012) *A guide to social return on investment*, London: SROI Network, www.socialvalueuk.org/app/uploads/2016/03/The%20Guide%20to%20Social%20Return%20on%20Investment%202015.pdf

Nutley, S., Walter, I. and Davies, H. (2003) 'From knowing to doing: a framework for understanding the evidence-into-practice agenda', *Evaluation*, 9(2): 125–48.

Nutley, S.M., Walter, I. and Davies, H.T.O (2007) *Using evidence: How research can inform public services*, Bristol: Policy Press.

Ovretveit, J. (1998) *Evaluating health interventions*, Maidenhead: Open University Press.

Parsons, D. and Thomas, R. (2015) *Evaluating the economic impact of social science*, Swindon: Economic and Social Research Council.

Parsons, D., Thomas, R., Strange, I. and Walsh, K. (2014) *Evaluating the impact of ESRC economic centres*, Swindon: Economic and Social Research Council, www.esrc.ac.uk/files/research/research-and-impact-evaluation/evaluating-the-impact-of-esrc-economics-centres/

Pawson, R. and Tilley, N. (1997) *Realistic evaluation*. London: Sage.

Pirracchio, R., Resche-Rigon, M. and Chevret, S. (2012) 'Evaluation of the propensity score methods for estimating marginal odds ratios in case of small sample size', *BMC Medical Research Methodology*, 12(70): 12–17.

Poth, C., Lamarche, M.K., Yapp, A., Sulla, E. and Chisamore, C. (2012) 'Towards a definition of evaluation within the Canadian context: who knew this would be so difficult?' *Canadian Journal of Program Evaluation*, 29(3): 1–18.

Ragin, C. (2000) *Fuzzy-set social science*, Chicago and London: The University of Chicago Press.

Rossi, P., Lipsey, M. and Freeman, H. (2004) *Evaluation: A systematic approach*, London: Sage.

St Leger, A., Schneiden, H. and Walsworth Bell, J. (1992) *Evaluating health services' effectiveness*, Bukingham: Open University Press.

Schatz, F. and Welle, K. (2016) *Qualitative comparative analysis: a valuable approach to add to the evaluator's 'toolbox'? Lessons from recent applications*, Centre for Development Impact Practice Paper No. 13, Brighton: Institute of Development Studies.

Schneider, C.Q. and Wagemann, C (2012) *Set-theoretic methods for the social sciences: A guide to qualitative comparative analysis (QCA)*, Cambridge: Cambridge University Press.

Schulz, K.F., Altman, D.G. and Moher, D. (2010) 'CONSORT 2010 statement: updated guidelines for reporting parallel group randomised trials', *British Medical Journal*, 340: c332.

Scottish Government (2011) *Guide 6: Contribution Analysis*, Social Science Methods Briefing Series (Revised May 2011), Edinburgh: Scottish Government, www.scotland.gov.uk/Topics/Research/About/Social-Research/Methods-Guides/Guide-6

Scriven, M. (1967) 'The methodology of evaluation', in R.W. Tyler, R.M. Gagne and M. Scriven (eds) *Perspectives of curriculum evaluation*, Chicago, IL: Rand McAlly, pp 54–73.

Scriven, M. (1991) *Evaluation theasaurus*, London: Sage.

Scriven, M. (1997) 'Truth and objectivity in evaluation', in E. Chelimsky and W. Shadish (eds) *Evaluation in the 21st century: A handbook*, Thousands Oaks, CA: Sage, pp 477–500.

Shadish, W.R., Cook, T.D. and Campbell, D.T. (2002) *Experimental and quasi-experimental designs for generalized causal inference*. Boston, MA: Houghton-Mifflin.

Shaw, I.F. (1999) *Qualitative evaluation*. London: Sage.

Sherman, L., Gottfredson, D., MacKenzie, D., Eck, J., Reuter, P. and Bushway, S. (1997) *Preventing crime: What works, what doesn't, what's promising*, Washington, DC: US Department of Justice.

Stern, E., Stame, N., Mayne, J., Forss, K., Davies, R. and Befani, B. (2012) *Broadening the range of designs and methods for impact evaluations: Report of a study commissioned by the Department for International Development*, London: DFID.

Stewart, D.W. and Kamins, M.A. (1993) *Secondary research: Information sources and methods*, Applied Social Research Methods: Vol. 4, London: Sage

Treasury Board of Canada Secretariat (2012) *Theory-based approaches to evaluation: Concepts and practices*, Ottawa, Canada: Centre of Excellence for Evaluation, www.tbs-sct.gc.ca/hgw-cgf/oversight-surveillance/ae-ve/cee/tbae-aeat/tbae-aeattb-eng.asp

United Kingdom Evaluation Society (2013) *Guidelines for good practice in evaluation*, London: UKES.

Weiss, C. (1979) 'The many meanings of research utilization', *Public Administration Review*, 39(5): 426–31.

Weiss, C. (1980) 'Knowledge creep and decision accretion', *Knowledge: Creation, diffusion, utilization*, 1(3): 381–404.

Weiss, C. (1998a), *Evaluation: Methods for studying programs and policies* (2nd edn), Upper Saddle River, NJ: Prentice Hall.

Weiss, C. (1998b), 'Evaluation in the 21st century', *Evaluation Exchange*, 4(2): 1–3.

White, H. and Phillips, D. (2012) *Addressing attribution of cause and effect in small 'n' impact evaluations: Towards an integrated framework*, Working Paper 15, International Initiative for Impact Evaluation, www.3ieimpact.org/media/filer_public/2012/06/29/working_paper_15.pdf

Annex A:
The ROTUR framework for managing evaluation expectations

1. Roles and responsibilities	
DO ...	**DO NOT ...**
- Start at the end: Who is the end user (any intermediaries)? How/when are they to be engaged in decision-making?	- Forget to identify internal/external procurement needs (may affect sign-off, funding limits, close/open tender, marketing etc.)
- Establish who has delegated responsibility for specification (including objective-setting, timetabling, resourcing and budgeting)	- Delay review of information/ data access needs (may affect timing; likely to need negotiation or disclosure agreements pre-start-up)
- Agree who manages all aspects of sign-off/commissioning and (if different) who project manages (including external contractors)	- Any internal roles (including project management) will need prioritised resourcing for evaluation to deliver on time
- Agree the focus of and how much method guidance to give to contractors pre-commissioning (and who will answer queries)	- Forget that credible findings may need independent analysis or validation (may affect resourcing and timing)

- Establish needs for any formal steering or progress review (what for, when and who)	- Forget to brief those recruited to steering on goals and agenda, their roles and any 'rules of engagement'
- If an internal evaluation, identify who fills what roles for direction, design, delivery/data collection, analysis/verification, reporting	- Ignore the need for an evaluation champion who will have the role of advocating change against findings (and with whom)

2. Outcomes needed of the evaluation	
DO ...	**DO NOT ...**
- Critically review your overarching aim statement for the evaluation: Is it clear, easily unambiguous and credible?	- Defer seeking wider agreement on the aims and objectives – aims must precede decisions on design and are not retrofitted
- Critically review the subsidiary objectives: Are they consistent with the rationale for what is being evaluated? Is it coherent with any logic chain/theory of change for the 'intervention'	- Forget to use objectives to clarify/ set out the specific areas where evaluation evidence is needed to aid decision-making
- Critically review the coverage of the objectives: Do they unnecessarily overlap or duplicate each other? If so, consolidate	- Use objectives (what/how evidence is to be used) to set out 'method' goals (ie. how to collect evidence) – method guidance (or prescription) follows objective–setting
- Use critical review to establish any gaps in aims/objectives: Is anything missing? How do aims etc. change to reflect any gaps?	- Hold back from asking for clarification or challenge of aims/ objectives – setting solid and appropriate expectations is the foundation of effective and usable evaluation

- Assess realism of aims and objectives; goals of the evaluation need to reflect the context, time and resources available	- Extend the aspiration for the evaluation beyond the needs of the aims and objectives – information and evidence is a tool and not just 'nice to know'
- Assess viability of aims and objectives: Are they consistent with likely information availability or evidence that can be gathered?*	

* An aide memoire on information availability

a) What evidence is (or is likely) to be available	Is past documentation being used (and is it subject to confidentiality constraints)? What available data/ useful evidence is readily available (when/lag times to collate)? Can it be harnessed (eg. are classifications/ time series/updating suitable? Is there baseline/comparative evidence? Etc.)
b) What 'accessible' sources (internal or external) can be used	Past evaluation/reviews/reports; contract compliance, funding or expenditure reports; beneficiary or participation records; in-programme management information; practice case studies etc.
c) Are they viable?	Data protection issues (identify/ personal information) may hold back accessibility/use; anonymity requirements. Is data already collated? Is it machine readable etc?
d) What are the gaps/residual information needs (for a–c)	Best focus for 'primary' evidence collection to update/extend/add to the available evidence set against aims and objectives of the evaluation?

3. Timing and delivery	
DO ...	**DO NOT ...**
- Take account of 'upstream' needs (eg. internal and/or external sign-off of specification), procurement notice period (eg. Official Journal of EU), marketing/tendering/commissioning decision-making lags etc.	- Forget to allow enough time also for potential contractors to produce viable tenders (2–4/5 weeks depending on needs)
- Build in 'engagement time' to liaise with stakeholders (ie. specification/ pre-start-up, during evaluation/ steering, pre-reporting including findings previews, review and sign-off of reports)	- Assume stakeholders are best held at 'arm's-length' until findings – earlier engagement brings challenges/ delays but can help later with credibility of findings
- Allow appropriate time for sensible measurement of outcomes (and impacts) – these may take time to be realised; compressed timeframes may miss/underrepresent achievements	- Skimp on time for design, testing and clearance of evaluation 'tools' – rushed design compromises information quality and reliability
- Allow sufficient time for gathering any new/additional evidence (eg. survey response/reminder time) and thorough analysis and interpretation by evaluators	- Forget that 'good' evaluators will need time for verification of the evidence they do collect – verification also adds to quality and credibility
- Build in time for staged/midpoint review (eg. via contract review or steering) – this is especially important for formative evaluations	- Underestimate the amount of time needed for staged review within 'formative' evaluations (especially where steering groups are involved)
- Allow for 'downstream' time after (draft) reporting to review, reflect on (consult?) and sign off evaluation before getting results/implications to decision makers etc.	- Underestimate time needed downstream to build credibility and confidence (and understanding) of findings among intermediaries, stakeholders/doubters) – evaluation utility may depend on this

4. Use and users of the evaluation	
DO ...	**DO NOT ...**
- Focus the evaluation approach, scope, timing and communication on the primary user(s). This will have been agreed from 'roles and responsibilities'. BUT ...	- Forget the secondary users ... appropriate engagement will help build credibility and also utility of the findings. Are there other (non-user) stakeholders who also need to be engaged?
- Clarify pre-specification how the evaluation findings are to be used: Are there any expectations of change/ improvement etc?	- Forget that different users (primary and secondary) may have different expectations of the evaluation and its utility – unrealistic expectations of change need to be countered/ conditioned for all
- Identify critical timings/decision-making points and align scope and approach to meet these (where appropriate)	- Forget that compressing the approach/scope to meet decision-making schedules may mean compromises need to be agreed with evaluation aims/objectives – re-engineer as appropriate
- Identify if there are critical 'user' intermediaries (people, functions or bodies) between whoever is accountable for the evaluation (and reporting its findings) and decision makers	- Underestimate the importance of champions/brokers of the evaluation findings (positive and negative) in influencing change – findings rarely speak for themselves among decision makers
- Identify sufficiently early if/what communication strategy is needed to bring findings/implications to the user-chain	

5. Resourcing the evaluation appropriately	
DO ...	**DO NOT ...**
- Recognise that resources are your budget, staff and time; these will vary with needs for internal or external evaluation	- Underestimate the staff resource and range of skills needed for internal evaluation; external advice or peer review may help build your confidence where the skills mix/ experience is limited
- Remember that 'appropriate' resourcing is led by scope, needs and expectations of evaluation – not availability of budget, staff and time. Limited resources may need compromises to aims etc.	- Be funding-led ('what can we do for the money?') – critically review if the budget available is appropriate for the aims and objectives (and/or proposed approach/scope)
- Appropriately resource project/ contract management – this takes time to do well. Does the allocated staff member have the necessary availability, skills and experience?	- Forget that project managers will need to balance the added demands of evaluation management with their other tasks/roles: Does the new role have clear prioritisation/sign-off?
- Are internal or partner interests/ functions 'bought in' to resourcing decisions (eg. is procurement able to support the necessary timetable?)	
- Set up appropriate review/steering arrangements pre-evaluation with clear briefing on roles/responsibilities to ensure engagement and continuity across evaluation	
- Ensure timing challenges are reflected in the agreed timetable – see all in 'Timing and delivery' (3) above	

Annex B:
Ready reckoner guide to experimentation choices in impact evaluation

	RCT/QE more viable when ...	RCT/QE less viable when ...
Budgetary availability for evaluation	- Internal evaluation: allocated staff resources/ staff release of suitably skilled and experienced project management evaluation team - External evaluation: substantial allocated budget or fixed resources for procurement of appropriate contractors for design, delivery, analysis and/or reporting	- Limited (or no) allocated staff resource or budget - Procurement constraints affecting financing (or contracting) with subcontracted expertise
Nature of programme or target intervention	- New policy/initiative - Distinct change in practice affecting participants - Non-complex and stable intervention environment	- Established/modified policy - Consolidating current activity - Multiple effect policy goals - Intervention environment not controllable for stability

Expected (likely) scale of programme impact	- Large expected effect - Distinctive effect relative to other changes taking place - Sustainable effect measurable in short timeframe	- Small expected effect - Complex environment (multiple confounding factors) - Long effect lead times or incremental impacts
Anticipated access and availability of appropriate data	- Appropriate data available on all individual participants - No data access constraints or constraints of the Data Protection Act?) - 'Isolatable' intervention - Data well fitted to intervention period/ classification needs - Comparative and control data – before-during-after intervention	- Data coverage not comprehensive - Data not adequately differentiated - Access constraints affecting some/all - Data not well fitted to intervention period; data lags - Summative data collection only - High levels of likely unintended consequences (eg. leakage)
Likely potential for comparator data/evidence	- Pilot or trial interventions preceding rollout - Phased rollout - Appropriate data for non-intervention groups - Objective selections within intervention/control - Minimised/measurable selection bias	- Full-scale rollout - Required data limited to pilot area, or inadequate comparisons - Ethical constraints to comparisons - Lack of control within intervention - Unstructured participant selections

Index

SOCIAL RESEARCH ASSOCIATION SHORTS

Series editors:

Patten Smith, Ipsos MORI Research Methods Centre

Ivana La Valle, University of East London &
independent consultant

The SRA Shorts Series is a research methods series in the Policy Press
Shorts format. They provide research practitioners, academics and
research users with short, high-quality and focused guides to specific
topics within the field of social research methods.

The series provides a voice for social research and practical guidance
for researchers to improve research quality. It focuses on social research
and practice, offering the chance to highlight the impact of research
on practice and policy and to draw attention to new and innovative
research methods.

Features of the series:

- Books will be 20–50,000 words long, equivalent to 50–150 pages.
- The content will be practical and accessible.
- Books will be of interest to an international audience.

Forthcoming:

Consulting skills for social researchers by Simon Haslam, May 2017

Printed and bound by CPI Group (UK) Ltd, Croydon, CR0 4YY

25/03/2025

14647337-0001